PROJECT RISE

8 WINNING HABITS TO BUILD THE BEST VERSION OF YOU

COLLIN HENDERSON

———————————

FOREWORD BY MIKE PRICE

*TWO-TIME PAC-12 COACH OF THE YEAR AND
NCAA NATIONAL FOOTBALL COACH OF THE YEAR*

PROJECT RISE

@COLLINHENDERSON

COLLIN HENDERSON

WWW.THECOLLINHENDERSON.COM

RISE

VERB
1. MOVE FROM A LOWER POSITION TO
A HIGHER ONE: GO OR COME UP
2. GET UP FROM LYING, SITTING, OR KNEELING

NOUN
1. AN UPWARD MOVEMENT:
AN INSTANCE OF BECOMING HIGHER
2. AN INCREASE IN AMOUNT, EXTENT,
SIZE, OR NUMBER

A RISING TIDE LIFTS ALL BOATS.
– JOHN F. KENNEDY, 1963

*TO MY TIDE, MY MOMENTUM, MY CHANGE AGENT,
MY LOVELY BRIDE, KENDRA. I WILL LOVE YOU FOREVER.*

FOREWORD

I had just become the head football coach at Washington State University in the spring of 1989. We were living in a rental home in Pullman, Washington, when we reconnected with the Henderson family. Jerry, Collin's dad, was a former teammate of mine back in the 1960s at WSU. Jerry was a fantastic quarterback and held many passing records for the Cougars.

He and his wife, Susan, and their two sons, Patrick and Collin, were visiting Pullman to see Susan's family. I was thinking they stopped by so our kids could meet each other; however, Jerry had videos of Collin playing Pop Warner football games. Wow! I have always taken pride in my recruiting skills and tried to be the first to identify a prospect, but the age of eight was even a little early for me!

Fast forward 10 years, and I am watching Collin's high school highlight tape. His dad was right. Wow, what a player, I thought. So, when Collin came to campus in the fall of his freshman year, everyone knew who he was and knew what a great athlete the Cougars were getting. He didn't take long to prove his worth, as he played as a true freshman wide receiver and punt returner for four great years. He had an excellent career in baseball for the Cougs also.

Like his father, he could really pass that football. Using trick plays, double passes, and reverse passes—as a wide receiver—he threw over a dozen passes and completed every one of them, including six for touchdowns! That's got to be an NCAA record. His leadership and attitude helped "will" our team to the 2003 Rose Bowl.

His teammates even voted him as the Frank Butler Award recipient—an honor awarded for spirited leadership. Collin was a tireless worker, great student, team player, great leader, and fierce competitor. In other words, he was the complete package.

That Rose Bowl team had some characters on it, though. But Collin wasn't a character; he had character. There's a big difference. In his four years of college, he was never in my office for doing something wrong. He probably wasn't perfect, but he was as close to it as anyone I've ever coached in my 45 years of coaching.

Him writing this book does not surprise me. Collin inspires people to be better than they are, which he did as a teammate. In this book, he will inspire you to be a better you, as well. That's what *Project Rise* has done for me.

This book has helped me reorganize my thinking and reexamine my life's priorities in an easy to understand system. Collin uses a lot of acronyms to describe his philosophy and his strategic plans. This system will make it easier for you to remember these principles.

After reading this book, you won't want to put it on your book shelf...you will want to use it as a workbook. Use this as a fun manual to keep by your side to help you refresh your plan. I recommend using this book every day to keep you inspired and on track. This is a success book. It's designed to help you become a better you. And remember: it's fun to be a better you! Enjoy *Project Rise*, and we look forward to seeing you experience a new you!

MIKE PRICE
TWO-TIME PAC-12 FOOTBALL COACH OF THE YEAR
NCAA NATIONAL FOOTBALL COACH OF THE YEAR

CONTENTS

WE RISE
BY LIFTING OTHERS

When I was coming up with the concept of this book, I knew I wanted to help a foundation or organization that inspires me. When it came down to aligning with a group, I thought of my former Washington State University (WSU) teammate and fellow wide-receiver (and roommate when we traveled) Devard Darling. Devard's story is pretty remarkable.

Devard was born an identical twin to brother Devaughn in the Bahamas. Devard and Devaughn were inseparable growing up, and both excelled in athletics—especially football. Living in Texas during their senior year in high school, Devard and Devaughn both committed to play football at Florida State University where they enrolled the following fall on scholarship. After competing that first year and playing in the Orange Bowl, Devaughn tragically died during offseason conditioning drills due to extertional sickling, a condition that can affect people with the sickle cell trait. Devard and his family were crushed. Grief stricken, Devard transferred to WSU, and was later drafted into the NFL. He has committed his life to honor his brother Devaughn through his As One Foundation.

Knowing Devard's passion for youth and serving others, I am donating partial proceeds from this book to the As One Foundation.

The As One Foundation's vision is to support and enhance youth development by providing youth-centered activities and opportunities to develop character, values, sportsmanship, responsibility, and positive relationships. Key initiatives include: sickle cell trait education, scholarships, athletic camps, the Darling Dash 5K Run, and Operation Hydration.

For more information, updates on events, and ways to help, visit: www.asonefoundation.org. Or search for #TraitWarrior on social media. Thank you for your support!

PROJECT RISE

INTRODUCTION
YOU GOT THIS!

Do you like dessert? Who doesn't? My personal favorite is chocolate cake with the raspberry filling. Many of you might already know this, but in order to make cake or dough RISE, you need to add the right ingredients, including a crucial change agent. What ingredient is this? It's baking soda, baking powder, or yeast. This book, *Project Rise* (accompanied by its counterpart, *Rise Journal*), is a similar type of change agent. And if used properly and consistently, it will be the necessary tool to take your life, goals, and fulfillment to the next level. In other words, it will help you RISE. After years of studying what brings success, and reflecting on my own life experiences, I have developed a recipe that will bring you the personal satisfaction that you have been craving. Cake, anyone?

If you are reading this book, I am assuming it's for a reason. You may have purchased it of your own accord (if so, thank you!), or maybe someone gifted it to you. Either way, you have reached a place in your life where you are seeking something greater. As the definition of RISE says, you are looking to move from a lower place to a higher one; to go or come up; to improve your current position; to increase in amount, extent, size, or number—in whatever it is you are seeking.

But in order to make this happen, something has to change. In order to RISE, you must get up from a lying, sitting, or kneeling position. The only way to change your emotion is with MOTION. In order to get satisfaction, you must take ACTION. If you are seeking improvement, you need MOVEMENT. This book will guide you to that end.

Before I get started and dig into the content I'm so excited to share with you, let me preface that you may have been exposed to similar concepts at some point in your life. Many of these strategies have been passed down from other great thinkers, leaders, and game-changers with more intelligence and experience than me. I am simply a devoted student. However, I believe *Project Rise* fills in many gaps and offers new ideas and approaches to complement many of the basic principles that you may have tried. The reality is, there is no magic method; it all comes down to execution and mastering the fundamentals—just like mastering layups and free throws before you attempt to master three-point shots in basketball.

Project Rise is designed to simplify your approach to being a better you. The information and habits I teach are packaged in a way that will help you do what you may have been putting off, have attempted and failed, or maybe have been too afraid to try. I help you master these crucial fundamentals in a fresh new way. But before we get there, my first challenge to you is this:

I WANT YOU TO IMAGINE.

Take a moment and imagine your future. I want you to remove any and all barriers and mental obstacles that have been holding you back from being the best version of you. Imagine living out your perfect day.

Where are you living?
What time are you waking up?
Who are you waking up next to?
What are you doing with your day?
Who are you spending your time with?
What career or lifestyle are you absolutely crushing?
What are you contributing to, and who are you helping?
What car are you driving?
What house are you living in?
How do you feel seeing your loved ones at the end of the day?

Take some time to picture a complete day where you are living a life of fulfillment and satisfaction, all playing to your passion and strengths. Take a few minutes to close your eyes, see these images, and feel these emotions. Do this exercise now...

●●●

Ok, now that you are back, I want you to imagine that same scenario, but imagine it EVEN BIGGER, with more abundance, and at a level that is 10 times more grand than what you just pictured.

●●●

This is the scene I want to help you create for your life and your future.

If it was easy for you to imagine your perfect day, then that's awesome; you are well on your way. However, some of you might have had a hard time picturing with clarity what a perfect day looks like for you, and that is okay. I am excited to help you maximize your potential as you begin a journey to capture what it is you are looking for, so you can not only visualize your perfect day, but create it also.

Below are eight habits that we will discuss. I love the fact that the number eight (8) is the same shape as the symbol of infinity—never-ending—similar to this process; it's ongoing. We are never a finished product, but constantly growing and learning and approaching each day and situation with a beginner's mindset, open to new ideas and change. Buddhist monk Shunryu Suzuki once wrote, "In the beginner's mind there are many possibilities, but in the expert's mind there are few." I challenge you to begin this journey with the same open mind, trust, and willingness to step outside your comfort zone as a beginner, not as a master.

These eight key habits transformed my life. To help you live these habits each day, I developed a journaling system that I include at the end of the book. This system is also available in a separate journaling book called *Rise Journal.* This tool will help you to keep the momentum going and continue to make these crucial habits a daily ritual. If you commit to this process, like I have, there is no doubt in my mind that you will create a system that brings out your best self.

HABIT 1: Master the art of goal setting and attainment.

The power of goal setting is time tested. I provide a simple framework that creates vision and purpose for your near and distant future.

HABIT 2: Create a system of writing down your thoughts, intentions, and goals (hence the Rise Journal).

It is scientifically proven that writing down your thoughts, feelings, and goals creates better results than not writing them down. I offer a system that helps with writing down your goals, action plan, and the "why" behind your vision. This approach will give you clarity and create a road map to be your best self.

HABIT 3: Practice gratitude.

The foundation of being your best self starts with being grateful. This one act is the first step of attracting more good in your life.

HABIT 4: Identify one key objective for your day.

Many people get distracted by tasks that do not even matter. Isolating one clear objective daily will help you win the day and gain the necessary momentum to achieve what you want.

HABIT 5: Give yourself daily affirmations.

What you say to yourself is 10 times more powerful than what anybody else can say to you. I give you tools to help you find your inner-voice, which will help you overcome negative thought patterns. The single act of owning your self-talk is one of the most crucial habits to becoming your best self.

HABIT 6: Learn something new every day.

The concept of learning can be found in two forms: 1) failing and learning from our mistakes and shortcomings, and 2) making a conscious effort to invest in our personal development by reading, listening, observing, or learning new information from mentors.

HABIT 7: Serve others.

We do not start living until we start giving. Living a life with a servant-leader mindset creates less stress, better health, more influence, and wealth—wealth in relationships and prosperity. The natural positive byproducts of service are undeniable.

HABIT 8: Visualize your goals and action steps daily, as if you have already accomplished them.

Your brain is a magnet. Visualizing your action and outcome goals as if you already have them creates a pathway for your body and soul to follow. Thoughts become things. When you establish the habit of filtering your mind to focus on positive outcomes instead of negative, you will take control of your life and attract abundance and success.

ARE YOU READY? IT'S TIME TO RISE.

PROJECT RISE

CHAPTER 1
WHY DID I CREATE PROJECT RISE?

EVEN THE DARKEST NIGHT WILL END AND THE SUN WILL RISE.
-VICTOR HUGO, LES MISÉRABLES

For most of my adolescent and young adult life, I lived like an iceberg: what you saw on top was not what was going on underneath. Above the surface, people saw a young man that appeared to have everything. In high school, I was homecoming king, all-state in football and baseball, the local newspaper's Athlete of the Year—heck, I was even voted "Dream Date" by my senior class.

The accolades continued into college, as I attended on scholarship to play both football and baseball at Washington State University. During my stint, I earned multiple all-conference and even all-American honors in academics, played in bowl games (including a Rose Bowl), was captain of the baseball team my senior year, and served as Student-Athlete Advisory Council vice president. Sounds like I had it made, right?

On the outside it may have seemed that way, but I was living a life filled with anxiety, stress, and insecurities; I was constantly comparing myself to others. In my own eyes, I was never good enough. Most of all, I feared failure. I put more weight into my perception of what others thought of me than my focus on simply being my best and enjoying the process.

I had what author Carol Dweck, PhD, describes in her book *Mindset: The New Psychology of Success* as a "fixed mindset." I received my validation and self-worth through outcomes and results only. Wins and losses were black and white; there were no shades of gray. Progress wasn't the focus, only winning was. When I played poorly or we lost, my self-esteem was deeply affected. My true potential was limited because I was paralyzed by trying to be perfect. It reached the point that, as a wide receiver, I even avoided going on deep pass patterns, afraid I would drop the ball. My self-confidence was shaky to say the least.

Another word for self-confidence is self-efficacy. There is a difference between self-efficacy and self-esteem, according to Martin Meadow's book *Confidence: How to Overcome Your Limiting Beliefs and Achieve Your Goals*. Self-efficacy, Martin writes, is "belief in your abilities"—like your ability to drive a car, cook, throw a baseball, or sing. We have self-efficacy in many different areas. Self-esteem, however, is belief in your own self-worth; your belief in yourself as a valuable human being. I, like many people, let performing poorly in specific areas in my life affect my self-esteem.

To make matters more challenging, my insecurity was heightened as a result of a mild stutter, which I tried, at all costs, to hide. Many people would never know, but my closest friends and family witnessed my lack of fluency on a consistent basis. I experienced many embarrassing moments, but the worst was definitely in speech class my sophomore year in high school. I remember feeling so much fear before I had to give a speech that it felt like my heart was going to beat out of my chest. Seriously, I was a nervous wreck!

I would get worked up, which impacted my performance and my self-esteem. The effect of these isolated events in a speech class spilled over socially. Many individuals have a fear of public speaking, but like most people—especially teenagers—I let that failure impact my self-worth.

A lack of self-efficacy in one area (like a mild stutter) should not determine one's self-image or validation. The goal is to have a "growth mindset," to look at failure not as a roadblock, but as a building block for success. Individuals with a growth mindset love a challenge and share the philosophy of Nelson Mandela: "I never lose. I either win, or I learn." As a high school sophomore, that wisdom was not yet embedded into my young psyche.

A fixed mindset followed me into my professional career, also. Even though I experienced success in medical sales, I rarely gave myself any margin for error. I achieved several promotions, award trips, even multiple Representative of the Year honors. Nevertheless, I often felt insecure, avoided many public speaking opportunities, and oftentimes was comparing myself to others. Without fail, I was found wanting. The stress of performing and constantly worrying about my image in front of my customers and peers was taxing. My anxiety hit an all-time high when our company made the decision to compensate the sales force on verbal tests over the phone, as well as written exams. This was definitely not good for me. My confidence surrounding speaking technically over the phone brought back my old anxieties. My fluency was affected, I wasn't performing well, and my self-esteem took a nosedive.

To add to the stress, I was promoted to account manager, a role I later discovered was not the right fit. I was calling on a specialty group of physicians that were hard to access. I am a people person who is energized by engaging with others. In my previous positions, I was seeing eight to ten customers a day. In this role, I was lucky to talk to one customer per day. I wasn't gaining traction, and my self-sabotaging thoughts made each day an uphill battle. I finally reached my tipping point.

Stressed and not sleeping well, my blood pressure elevated into the high 140s. My doctor prescribed me blood pressure medicine. Knowing this, I started to look for outlets to lower my stress. I tried Transcendental Meditation, but that didn't seem to work. I met with a counselor several times to discuss what I was going through, but we didn't connect, and I didn't see growth. I reached a breaking point; I knew I needed to get out. I needed fresh scenery.

God's timing is all-knowing and perfect. He threw me a lifeline that changed my life. My manager gifted me a book to start a new year, *Positive Intelligence*, by Shirzad Chamine.

21

We all suffer with bouts of self-doubt and occasional negative thinking. There are always two sides in our brain duking it out, fighting over "yes I can" or "no I can't." Unfortunately, often times I was on the losing end of this internal war, in both my athletic and professional careers. *Positive Intelligence* helped me identify that we all have mental saboteurs in our brain, and if we can realize that this internal judge is a liar, a fraud, and a fake, we can stay focused on positive thoughts, concentrate on our strengths, and keep our minds honed in on the task at hand.

This newfound knowledge gave me the confidence and the tools to nail my interview with a Fortune 500 medical device company and jumpstart a three-year period of enlightenment and self-discovery.

After joining this company, I was assigned a trainer and mentor named Frankie Pretzel (is that not the coolest name you have ever heard?). Frankie was a seasoned veteran in the medical device industry who had won multiple awards and was very successful. Frankie was an optimist. He knew the power of positive thinking and the effect it has on our lives. He explained to me a concept I had never been exposed to: the Law of Attraction. Basically, the Law of Attraction is a concept that is summed up as simple as this: thoughts become things. What we think about and visualize the most is usually manifested somehow, someway, whether negative or positive. Frankie gave me a long list of books to read that kick-started my obsession with what creates success. This fresh start and exposure to new ideas, thoughts, and concepts—all dealing with generosity, gratitude, self-belief, and visualization—helped me create the momentum I was searching for my entire life.

These past several years have been nothing short of amazing. By committing to personal development, surrounding myself with mentors and positive people—by shifting my mindset from being fixed to seeking growth, self-love, and gratitude—I've reached a place of peace and rest in my soul I have never felt before. My wife Kendra and I now live in our dream home. I've achieved accolades as a top sales performer in my company, as well as a sales trainer. I've been writing about my journey in my blog *Project Rise* (www.theCollinHenderson.com), as well as speaking to audiences, schools, and athletic teams about the power of one's mindset. I've finally actualized my potential and purpose on this planet. My passion is to be a student of what brings success: to learn it, understand it, apply it, and pass it along to as many people as possible.

MY MISSION IN LIFE IS TO HELP PEOPLE BECOME THE BEST VERSION OF THEMSELVES.

I am truly honored to help you through your journey of finding your purpose and giving you the tools and strategies that will take your life to the next level.

This book and journal have been carefully crafted over several years of studying what the most successful people have done and continue to do to create happiness, relationships, health, wealth, and prosperity. During this time of research and learning, I have found that there are certain patterns, rituals, and habits that create this success. I've spent thousands of hours listening to audio books and podcasts. I have read tons of books from key thought leaders, life strategists, and the wealthy—wealthy in relationships, in spirit, and in finances. I have watched and listened to countless videos on YouTube, listening intently and taking notes nonstop. I have reflected on my life—my achievements and my failures. I have gone through notebook after notebook documenting these success secrets that, when you break them down, are actually quite simple.

Complexity is the enemy of execution. Knowing this, I have trimmed it down to make it easy for you to process, actualize, and execute. Ideas are great, but they are meaningless without execution. Call me your "execution coach."

The first part of the book deals with creating a clear vision and plan to achieve your dream. I'll help you define your goals, identify reasons why you want to achieve them, and give you tools to create an action plan that solidifies into habit. In the later chapters,

I'll review the main elements that will make up your *Rise Journal*. I encourage you to take up a system of writing each day. Even if it's just a couple of minutes. My *Rise Journal* system will make it very easy for you. If you learn and practice these principles daily, you undoubtedly will RISE! This system is based on the acronym: GOALS V.

G - GRATITUDE
O - OBJECTIVE
A - AFFIRMATION
L - LEARN
S - SERVE

V - VISUALIZE

By learning from my descent and RISE, I hope you discover something inside of you that unleashes a powerful force that will take you to experiences, levels, and heights you have never seen before. Invest and trust this process, and I believe you will go farther than you once thought possible.

HABIT #1: SET GOALS

THIS SECTION IS ALL ABOUT REVERSE ENGINEERING THE BEST VERSION OF YOU. CHAPTERS 2, 3, AND 4 WILL HELP YOU SPECIFY YOUR GOALS AND IDENTIFY A CLEAR VISION FOR YOUR LIFE. BY BEGINNING WITH THE END IN MIND, YOU WILL CREATE CLARITY AND PURPOSE—TWO ESSENTIALS FOR EXCELLENCE AND BUILDING YOUR BEST SELF.

CHAPTER 2
WHAT DO YOU WANT?

WHEN YOU HAVE CLARITY OF INTENTION, THE UNIVERSE
CONSPIRES WITH YOU TO MAKE IT HAPPEN.
-FABIENNE FREDRICKSON

The purpose of *Project Rise* is to create a breakthrough in your life, much like I experienced several years ago. Not just a one-time breakthrough, but making the single most important investment you can make in life—and that is investing in you. Once you realize you have the power to take ownership of your happiness, ownership of your achievement, and fully understand that you have the unspeakable POWER OF CHOICE, you won't be stopped. According to pioneering American psychologist Julian Rotter, this concept is called having an *internal locus of control*. Meaning you have control over your life. Your beliefs, thoughts, actions, and habits dictate the life you create for yourself. No one else is driving this ship but you.

People who have an *external locus of control* believe that they are a creation of their environment. They believe in luck and chance. This concept couldn't be farther from the truth. This is my thought on luck: the harder you work, the luckier you'll get. Can you think of anybody you know who has an external locus of control?

Once you decide to take ownership of your thoughts, personal development (my favorite), and your actions—you will have the clarity to attack life and stop sitting on the sidelines. But you must,

I mean must, take action.

THE VERY WORD ACT STANDS FOR: ACTION CHANGES THINGS.

Don't be the person who looks back and regrets that they did not take action, wishing you would have done something different. Today's the day to take action to be a better you. It all starts with the right mindset and the correct tools and strategies to take you there—that's what this book and journaling system is going to do for you. But, before we get there, I have a couple questions I'd like to ask.

TWO QUESTIONS

In order to become the best version of you, I want you to think about this: What do you want? What is holding you back?

WHAT DO YOU WANT?

Let's start with the first question. It's pretty basic, but I don't think many people really take the time to dig deep and explore their true desire and passion. I've found that a significant number of people are not able to identify what it is they specifically want. Their answer is oftentimes masked by what they think their partner, parents, friends, or society wants to hear. So, what do you want? Is it better relationships, health, financial security, or a new career? Whatever it is for you, it's time to cut the B.S., identify it, and go after it.

Lisa Nichols is an author, media personality, corporate CEO, and one of the world's most requested motivational speakers. She describes how we need to think of goal setting like going to a restaurant. When you sit down, look at your menu, decide what you want, then tell the waitress your order, you are expecting without any doubt that you'll receive that order.

This is the first key step in attaining the place in the future that I asked you to imagine earlier in the book.

If you are able to pinpoint exactly what it is you desire, with extreme clarity, while believing with all your heart that it will come true, you can achieve it. The process will definitely take time and an insane amount of hard work, but if you can identify specifically want you want, visualize it, and take action, you can achieve anything.

For example, I had the good fortune to meet five-time Olympic medalist—four time gold medalist—Janet Evans. As a 12-year-old girl, Janet's life changed forever. Living in Southern California, she attended the opening ceremonies of the 1984 Olympics in Los Angeles. After seeing all the pageantry, fanfare, and excitement surrounding the Olympic athletes, she knew with crystal clarity what she wanted to do with her life. From that day forward, she devoted every ounce of her being to becoming an Olympic swimmer.

With a clear vision, she told her 22-year-old swim coach what she wanted. Her coach, said, "OK, Janet, if that is what you want, this is what you must do." He then set up a plan that consisted of waking up at 4:30 a.m., swimming 12 miles a day in the pool, completing 30 minutes of push-ups and sit-ups each day, and sticking to a strict meal plan. Janet didn't mind. For the next four years, she trained six days a week, year-round with one goal: make the Olympic Team.

Equipped with a passionate goal, nothing was going to stop her. With her clear intention, purpose, and insane work ethic, not only did Janet make the team, but she broke a world record and won three gold medals in the 1988 Olympics in Seoul, Korea. All this from a young and undersized 18-year-old, just five feet four inches and 99 pounds!

Needless to say, Janet's story really inspired me and reinforced the power of having a clear goal.

Now, let's go back to the analogy that achieving your goals is like ordering your favorite meal at a restaurant. But let's take it to the next level. Instead of simply ordering, this time, you'll be the chef and the creator. Instead of relying on others or external forces to get what you want, you'll be in control. It's like mastering

29

your perfect meal in the kitchen—you source your best ingredients, spend your time crafting the recipe, and after all is said and done, you get to enjoy what you have worked so hard for. That means reaping the rewards of all your efforts—a delicious meal that you created.

Just like Janet Evans, you too can serve up something measurable and life-changing.

To reach this maximum potential though, it is critical not to respond to the question—what do you want?—with an answer you think other people want to hear. So many people are living a surface life; they are not digging deep and cutting through the crap. If you have been lying to yourself, and there are many reasons we do, it's time to stop! What is it that you want? Be authentic. Be honest. Life is too short to fail to identify and go after what you truly want and desire. It's time to get cooking!

WHAT IS HOLDING YOU BACK?

Here's the challenge: if it were as easy as visualizing what you want, then everyone would be rolling in yachts, spinning on dubs, and featured on MTV's Cribs (do they still even make that show?). However, oftentimes there is an obstacle that holds us back and keeps us from either attempting or accomplishing our goals. I am not talking about external challenges. I'm talking about mastering your inner game, taking control of your mindset. Most of the time this obstacle, roadblock, or adversity takes the form of fear—fear of judgement, embarrassment, failure, ridicule, scarcity, safety, or maybe even success.

If you follow the origin of stress or pressure, it will take you down a winding road that leads to fear. The human brain is designed to survive; it is not designed to thrive. That is where filtering your thoughts and taking ownership of your self-talk comes into play. I want to help you see yourself in a different light. You have everything it takes to do or be whatever you want to be. You just need to see it first. This process starts by addressing the origin of your stress.

30

I want you to retool your brain to change how you look at fear. There are definite and understandable sources of stress and fear: health, protection, and safety, for starters. But, many times, FEAR is False Evidence Appearing Real. Fear is a physical response to a mental threat. Fear is all about allowing anticipation to get the best of you...just like I used to do before speaking in public.

Many operate in a place of fearful anticipation, which holds them back from stretching and growing. Instead, let's use anticipation to serve us rather than allowing anticipation to hold us down as we expect the worst. Believe that the best is yet to come and anticipate growth and excitement by trying something new or different.

DON'T LET FEAR BE A HEADWIND.
ALLOW FEAR TO BE A TAILWIND.

Imagine if Adele gave in to her fear of performing in front of a live audience (she's said she often suffers from severe stage fright). If she gave into her fear, Adele would miss out on achieving her true potential, and the world would miss out on her wonderful gift. However, this Grammy-winning and multiplatinum-selling artist fights through the fear. She uses it as energy—and is handsomely rewarded for it.

Unlike Adele, people who let fear dictate their behavior live a life of mediocrity and do not reach their full potential. When we are faced with FEAR, we have two choices:

FORGET EVERYTHING AND RUN
OR
FACE EVERYTHING AND RISE!

Let me encourage you that you are enough. You have what it takes. No one is immune to fear, worry, or doubt. I do not care if you're Beyonce, Odell Beckham, Jr., or Bill Gates. We all go through moments of self-doubt and fear. However, people who accomplish their dreams, are able to RISE above with just 10 minutes, one minute, or even 10 seconds of courage. Once you get past that initial first step, you'll realize that it's not that bad.

My life didn't change until I DECIDED to face my insecurities and fear of public speaking. I had to open up to people I trusted; then I took action by enrolling in speech therapy and Toastmasters. To this day, I still work on my speaking and communication skills and challenge myself to be uncomfortable daily.

When speaking to audiences, I sometimes compare fear to poop...or changing a baby's diaper for the first time (oh yes, I'm going there—I have four kids, five years old and under). When we had our first child, Baylor, I would lean back as far as I could and gingerly change his diaper. It felt uncomfortable, and I didn't know what I was doing. Now that we are on baby number four, I'm like the NASCAR pit crew...I'm all in, changing that diaper 200 miles an hour! The more you do something, the less fear-inducing it becomes—like my example of being stressed about public speaking. The act of doing what I used to fear the most now brings me the most joy.

IF YOU DO WHAT YOU FEAR THE MOST, THERE IS NOTHING YOU CANNOT DO.

Without struggle, you will not build strength. Our greatest promise lies within our greatest pain. Be vulnerable enough to make your mess your message and talk to someone about what is holding you back. We all are dealing with obstacles in our path to being our best self; whether it's addiction, guilt, an unhealthy relationship, past failures, or fear of their future...you are not alone. Because we are human, we all have problems and challenges. These trepidations will not diminish until you talk to someone about what issues you are dealing with.

This roadblock for some of you might not be one fear that you can single out. It might be a story that you have been telling yourself over and over, one that might sound like this: "I am not talented enough. I am not smart enough. I am a product of my environment. No one around me has ever made anything out of their lives, so I probably won't either." Or maybe you've been listening to or caring too much about someone else's opinion of you. Please know that opinions are not facts—they are simply someone else's opinions. It's time to break this mental routine and rewrite your story.

Let me ask you right now: <u>WHAT IS HOLDING YOU BACK FROM BEING THE BEST VERSION OF YOU?</u> This is one of the most important steps you must take in order to be your best self. My dad always taught my brother Patrick and me not to run away from adversity, but to ATTACK IT. It's time that you AT-TACK your fear or negative internal story and make it your bitch (pardon my French)! Start small, and slowly address your biggest roadblock. The more you expose yourself and address the area in your life that is causing stress, you will become more confident and over time, you will be well on your way to achieving your goals. Here are six steps to take right now to aggressively go after what has been holding you back.

STEP 1: Identify Your Fear

Identify specifically what it is that you fear or have been avoiding. What causes you not to act because of the fear of embarrassment, failure, pain, uncertainty, or your image (don't get me started on social media)? Your own negative thought pattern or internal story might be the culprit. Identify the barrier that is limiting or keeping you from being your best.

STEP 2: Tell Someone

Just this simple act of telling someone you trust about what you are dealing with will release some of the tension and lift some of the weight you have been carrying.

STEP 3: Guard Your Thoughts

Recognize when your internal judge pops up and tries to tell you that you are not worthy or good enough (this was one of my biggest challenges.). Tell that judge to shut up! This is not the real you. Give yourself positive affirmation and uplifting self-talk to overcome your doubts.

STEP 4: Create A Mantra

Come up with a word or a phrase that snaps your mind back on track when automatic negative thoughts appear. (Some I've used have been: "go deep," "compete," "let's go," or "I got this"). The brain has 35 automatic thoughts per minute and 50,000 thoughts per day. Your mantra word or phrase will help you refocus your brain to have the courage to keep moving in a positive direction.

STEP 5: Change A Pattern

Take the actions necessary to change the pattern that has kept you in this negative state. Create a new routine that will set in motion the steps and the actions necessary to turn your hardship into happiness. I used to replay my failures over and over in my head, whether I dropped a pass in football, I messed up when speaking in public, or I butchered a sales call. This thought pattern definitely held me back. It wasn't until I stopped these negative thought patterns that my confidence and courage grew. Instead, I replayed past success and visualized positive outcomes (e.g., making the play, nailing my speech, or closing an account because of a fantastic sales call). This made a huge difference.

When you change your pattern and take action, remember to focus on quantity not quality. The more you do something, the less scary it gets. But you need to change your routine and face your fear. Nothing will change until this critical step is addressed. I hope this book and journal will help you change this paralyzing pattern.

STEP 6: Face Your Fear!

This is the last and most important step to set your goals in motion. You will not grow and progress until you get out of your comfort zone and stretch yourself. No one is invulnerable to worry or stress. True champions have the courage to face their fears, and when they do, they build strength, power, and confidence. Once they've taken this step, most usually say, "It wasn't that bad."

In Don Joseph Goewey's book, *The End of Stress*, he reports a study from Cornell University in which subjects were told to write down their worries for two weeks and then track which actually came true. Participants found that the vast majority of their worries (85%) never came to fruition. Of the 15% that did actually happen, it often wasn't as bad as they'd imagined. In fact, 79% of the time, participants reported that things went better than expected.

Stop telling yourself, "I could never do that." I'm here to encourage you that, "Yes you can!" I have learned this to be true in many aspects of my life, from starting a podcast to speaking to a new audience to calling on a tough account in my medical sales role. Doing something new that is outside of our comfort zones is usually not as bad as our brain often makes it out to be. Keep this in mind as you create a vision for what you want to achieve in the short term and long term.

My next chapter will give you more space to write down and answer in more detail the first question: "What do you want?" Use the space below to think about and identify what is it that you want and what is holding you back. Fill in the steps that I mentioned above to ATTACK whatever it is that is hindering you from being the best version of you.

As legendary life coach Zig Ziglar used to say, "Don't be a wandering generality. Be a meaningful specific." Take a moment to think about the person you want to become and the life you want to live. What do you want? ???
Write it down in the space below:

Now take some time to identify what force or forces are keeping you from RISING to this place. Answer these four questions below.

What is holding me back?

_____

Who can I talk to about this and when will I do this?

_____

What is a word or phrase I can say that will switch my mindset when my programmed negative thoughts or doubts appear? This will be my mantra or slogan that will fuel my action.

_____

What is the one pattern in my life I must address that will set in motion transformational change?

_____

RISE REVIEW

The first step to being the best version of you is to answer these two basic questions:

- What do I want?
- What is holding me back?

Break down any barriers, thoughts, or past failures that have been keeping you down. Create clarity and purpose in your life by specifying a clear goal that you'd like to achieve. Just this simple act will create momentum, excitement, and energy to take the necessary steps to make it happen.

Often times, the first step to reaching your potential is to address the source of your stress, nervousness, or anxiety. The origin of these emotions usually can be tracked to some sort of fear. When faced with a challenge, adversity, or fear, we must not run and hide, but attack it head on. Follow these 6 steps:

- Identify the source
- Tell someone
- Guard your thoughts
- Create a mantra to keep your mind on track
- Change a pattern and create a new routine
- Face your fear

Remember: IF YOU DO WHAT YOU FEAR THE MOST, THERE IS NOTHING YOU CANNOT DO! This is a crucial initial step to turning your dreams into reality.

CHAPTER 3
GPS-GOAL PERFORMANCE SYSTEM

WITHOUT A GOAL, YOU CAN'T SCORE.

-CASEY NEISTAT

I love acronyms. I enjoy the puzzle of taking a word with multiple letters and piecing together a larger meaning. I'm about to share a few powerful acronyms with you—so get ready.

This is your task. It centers around one of the most impactful forces for creating achievement and growth, and that is having GOALS. If you are taking this journey of life without a clear goal, it's like traveling to an unknown destination without a road map or navigation system—you'll definitely get lost. However, when you are operating with a clear goal, it's like navigating your journey with a GPS, only this one isn't used to help navigate your car; this system is used to navigate your life.

This GPS stands for Goal Performance System. If you are not operating with this system, you'll most likely take several wrong turns, hit a few dead ends, and your journey will take much longer before you arrive at your desired destination.

The software of this GPS is the GOALS V system which is the journaling format I use (Gratitude. Objective. Affirmation. Learn. Service. Visualize). GOALS hold the power to transform your current condition into the one that you imagined at the beginning of the book.

GENESIS OF MY GOAL

This book is a manifestation of a goal that I shared with my friend Chad Veach, who is a pastor of an amazing church in Los Angeles called Zoe LA. It was September of 2013, and Chad was invited to speak at a church in Miami. He usually brings a guest on these trips, and he invited me to come along. While in South Beach, hanging out at the pool on a gorgeous sunny day, I remember having this feeling come over me that I wanted to write a book. I had no idea what the topic was going to be, but I felt a gentle whisper and push inside encouraging me to write. After ordering our lunch pool side, I shared this desire with Chad. Being the kind and supportive friend that he is, he said, "That's awesome Collin, I'd read your book." That moment right there was the seed that planted the goal of being an author. But like seeds, goals take time to grow.

After that moment, nothing happened on the book-writing front for two years, but a great deal had transpired in my life. Kendra and I bought a new house and had our second child, Bellamy. I switched companies and experienced tremendous growth and satisfaction in my career—finally. After the experience of going through a rough patch professionally and personally (as I shared in Chapter 1), I survived that turbulence with a better understanding of what it takes to thrive. Through this experience, I felt it was time to write and share my thoughts with the intent to help people.

I remember having this strong urge of wanting to make a positive impact on others. It was December of 2015, and I had just wrapped up probably the happiest year of my life. I was clicking on all cylinders personally and professionally—our marriage and home life was flourishing—I was winning awards and accolades at work, and we were earning an income that exceeded anything that we had ever earned before. With this progress, I finally had enough confidence to be vulnerable and share my story.

I'll never forget having this conversation with my wife Kendra. It was a dark December evening, and I was sitting on the floor of our living room, while she was on the stairs. We had the fire going, the kids were in bed, and we were enjoying some quiet time just talking to each other (those of you with young children can appreciate these peaceful moments.). I opened up to her about how I wanted to write a book (again, not having a title or outline of what I wanted to write about). I shared that I wanted to leave a legacy and do something bigger than simply working a nine to five job. I wanted to help people RISE and experience growth similar to my experience. She gave me some great wisdom.

Kendra runs a successful home business as a graphic designer and blogger. However, her success didn't happen overnight, but through several years of trial and error and slow consistent growth. She has a popular blog (HEN & CO.) that gets tens of thousands of hits per month. Having this experience and success under her belt, she advised me, "Why don't you start a blog first?" She added, "This will help you find your voice and establish an audience." I knew I married her for more than just her looks. That was how my blog, *Project Rise*, was created (she helped me come up with my blog's name, too. I am so thankful I married up!).

The journey of writing a blog allowed me to practice. I practiced my writing style, research strategies, putting my ego aside, and sharing my blemishes, flaws, and mistakes. It provided me a platform to share my theories on a variety of topics, and most importantly, my blog helped me find my voice. A key element of goal attainment is the understanding that it takes a great deal of practice, trial and error, and multiple failures to actualize your goal. My first few blog posts were painful to write and painful to read too. It had been 10 years since I completed graduate school, and my writing was pretty rusty.

Over time though, I developed a process and a style, and my writing went from being a chore, to something I truly enjoyed.

All this practice and refinement were great, but I still didn't have a title or a specific topic for my book. I had a few ideas and concepts, but nothing concrete. Then, out of nowhere, exactly three years to the month after my conversation with my friend Chad, where I shared that I wanted to write a book someday, the vision flashed at me like neon lights in Times Square. I was lying in my daughter Bellamy's bed snuggling one Saturday morning (what can I say? I'm a sucker for a good snuggle), and I saw this image in my head:

GOALS

The acronym of GOALS hit me like a 90 mile per hour fastball. I thought, "I got it: GOALS!" GOALS: Gratitude, Objective, Affirmation, Learn, and Service (I added the V for Visualize a few days later). These strategies as a collective group are what helped me get to this place in my life—feeling fulfilled with passion and purpose. From my descent, and then RISE, I practiced all of those things daily, but had yet to come up with a simple format of packaging them all together in a system that can be utilized collectively.

When this vision hit me, I thought, "These are the main habits that I have utilized these past few years." I consistently wrote down my goals and action plan. I made gratitude a daily practice to prime my spirit. I clarified my main objective for the day. I changed my mindset and practiced affirmations daily. I actualized the power of investing in my personal development by learning something new every day. I understood the life-changing benefits that serving others creates. I believed that by visualizing my goals as if I already had them, I would attract what I wanted in life.

The next step, I thought, was to piece these life-changing practices together into a simple system of writing them down.

Pumped and fired up, the next thing I did was go to Target and buy a journal. I didn't buy just one, but several. For the next several months (and still to this day) I used this system daily to create intention and to document my journey. I loved this system so much and saw what a profound impact it had on me, I wanted to share it with as many people as I could. Everyone was fair game: friends, family, colleagues, customers, and even strangers. I shared this system with anyone who had ears. I even gave many people a journal—those extras I bought at Target. I told them my story, and offered this approach. I wanted to test my theory and see how this journaling system could help other people RISE just like me, even if they were content with their lives.

After some time passed, the positive feedback I received on the *Rise Journal* validated my theory. This format helped the people in my sample group create a target, a plan, and a clearer purpose each day. Whether it was combating stress, feeling unfulfilled at work, ungratefulness, a relationship issue, or the lack of a fitness routine, this system seemed to improve at least one key area in their lives. This news felt better than selling any medical device to a doctor because I was directly impacting someone's life for the better—either emotionally, spiritually, or physically.

This response filled my cup like no other. With this reassurance, I knew it was game-time. And here you are, reading a goal of mine that was planted several years ago. This is so cool! It took hundreds of hours of watering, nurturing, pruning, and working hard to fight storms, but this goal has blossomed into something I am very proud of. You can create a similar story, too.

As you can see in this example, some of our biggest goals do not happen right away, but take a great deal of work. Patience is a superpower that few possess. No one said it would be easy, but that it would be worth it. Start with a goal and have the perseverance and persistence to see it through. Use this system to help you in your journey—just like a GPS device. By setting a goal in your mind, your subconscious will give you the coordinates on how to get there. This system will help navigate the path to your ultimate purpose—no matter how long it takes.

RETICULAR ACTIVATING SYSTEM

When you set a clear goal that you are passionate about, similar to my example above, your brain will act like a heat-seeking missile. Even though you are often chasing a moving object, your subconscious will find a way to hone in on the steps and actions necessary to hit your target. This is because at the base of the brain stem lies a cluster of nerve cells called the reticular activating system (RAS). According to the article, *Exploring the Neuroscience and Magic Behind Setting Your Intent – And Creating an Optimal Future for Yourself,* by Kris Hallbom and Tim Hallbom from the *NLP Institute of California,* "The RAS takes instructions from your conscious mind, and passes them onto your subconscious mind."

The authors add, "Setting your intent plays a key role in encouraging your subconscious mind to bring forth a desired goal, as well the most optimal future."

We are constantly barraged by countless stimuli vying for our attention. The main function of our RAS is to determine what gets noticed and what doesn't—it serves as the brain's radar system—to help filter what we should pay attention to and what we shouldn't.

Similar to a GPS device, once you have your goal locked in, your brain creates a category in your RAS, and you start to notice everything that will help you reach your destination and accomplish your goal. When I became serious about writing my first book, I immediately starting noticing in more detail everything about books: who the authors were, what the layouts looked like, how they were structured, who the publishers were, if it was self-published, what the cover art looked like, what punctuation was used. When I read other books, or listened to podcasts, my content became almost effortless. Because of my clear vision and GOALS outline, I could easily place stories, anecdotes, and new information I learned into my categories.

Once you have a clearly defined goal, it allows your RAS to go to work for you and help you stay focused on what's necessary to reach it.

ONE PERCENT

OK, I can guess what you might be thinking: "I know all about goal setting. I have heard this all before. Tell me something I don't know."

I am fully aware that I am not the first person to highlight the power and significance of goal setting. Many before me have and many after me will continue to preach the importance of creating a vision and having purpose in your life. However, let me ask you these questions: *Are you absolutely crushing it in your field right now? Are you waking up each day with excitement and passion? Are you fulfilled?*

Reflect right now. *Have you written down your goals for today, this month, this year, and for the distant future?* My guess is that only 10% of the people who are reading this book can answer "yes." Many may create a goal, but most have not taken the time to write it down and look at it every day.

My next question is this: *Have you spent the time to write down what actions and steps you must take to make your goals a reality?* I'd say the percentage of those who answered "yes" is now down to 5%.

Lastly, and in my opinion, most importantly: *Have you spent time thinking about your reasons for creating your goals?*

Motives matter. Being able to identify why you want these goals, how they will make you feel when you accomplish them, and how this achievement will affect you and those around you, is what I call WHY-Power. Having WHY-Power is essential to get you out of bed, off the couch, and into action. WHY-Power is vital to turning your dreams into reality.

Now, the percentage of people who can answer "yes" to all of these might have dropped to 1%. That means, in all reality, only 1% of the people reading this book have the BIG 4 of Goal Setting, or G4, as I like to call it. I like calling this approach the G4 because, like a G-IV Jet, it's a vehicle that can fly and take you wherever it is you want to go. However, this G4 is not some esoteric approach only for the ballers and the wealthy. Anyone can fly high on the G4! Turning your goals into reality takes only four simple steps.

THE BIG 4 OF GOAL SETTING (THE G4):
1. Create a GOAL
2. Commit it to PAPER
3. Develop and execute an action PLAN
4. Identify your WHY

45

So, what sets the 1% apart from everyone else? According to *Fortune Magazine* and writer Geoffrey Smith, 1% of the world's population owns half of the world's wealth. Are you that 1%? Sometimes, the 1% is vilified in the media as being greedy and self-serving. But what if you became one of the 1%, and you did it differently. What if you used your power and resources to become an agent for change? Do you know what it takes to be in the 1%? After five years of researching the elite wealthy, Thomas C. Corley listed 13 habits of self-made millionaires. Guess what? Goal Setting made the list. The top 1%, the wealthiest self-made men and women, exercise the power of goal setting, and you should too. Extraordinary people do what others are not willing to do—even the small things that many overlook. Do not miss out or think you are too big-time, established, set in your ways, or too cool for this. Not having a vision and plan is planning to fail. How can you hit your target if you've nothing to aim for?

Below is a summary of the four elements of goal setting, which I'll discuss in more detail in the following chapters:

CREATE A GOAL

It all boils down to fundamentals. You must master the fundamentals before you can achieve greatness. Ask anyone in martial arts, the military, sports, business, medicine, engineering, or music; it's all about the FUNDIES! Michael Jordan once said, "Get the fundamentals down and the level of everything you do will RISE."

Goals provide you with a road map and internal GPS—a *Goal Performance System*—that gives you clarity and purpose. Living life without goals is like going to the grocery store without a shopping list: you'll waste time wandering all over the store, and who knows what you'll come home with.

Like many people, I have some months when I go through the motions and forget to write down a specific goal that I want to accomplish. I get caught up in the many other things that I juggle with my life: my marriage, coaching, spending time with my family, writing my blog, and speaking to groups—oh, and my eight to five medical sales job.

When periods like this come up, I do my best to recognize that I'm operating on cruise control, and I force myself to snap out of it. By realizing that I didn't set a specific intention for myself in a given time period, I quickly go back to the basics and ask myself this simple question again, "What is it that I want to accomplish?" I think about it, decide on an outcome and the key actions I need to take, and then write them down. Once this happens, I feel like I'm back operating within my GPS. When I revisit my coordinates, my performance and satisfaction always RISE.

When you're living a life filled with goals, it's important to have different stages or milestones along the way. These goals will be your compass and guide for your life. This is nothing you haven't heard before, but I will teach you this basic success principle in a way that makes it easy to zero in on what you need to focus on and document.

COMMIT IT TO PAPER

Putting your goals to paper is like signing a contract with yourself. Dr. Gail Matthews, a psychology professor at Dominican University in California, performed a goal setting study, which included 267 participants. She found that people are 42% more likely to achieve their goals just by writing them down. By taking the time to think through your goals and to write them down—as specifically as possible, which is key—you are creating clarity and mental imaging that leads to actualization. Consider the alternative: a few random thoughts squashed by your inner critic.

DEVELOP AND EXECUTE AN ACTION PLAN

Having goals and writing them down is the first step to being the best version of you. This clarity will create something inside you that drives you to come up with ideas about HOW to get there. But here's the thing: you can't achieve your goals and dreams just by writing them down and doing nothing. You must take ACTION!

47

AVERAGE IN = AVERAGE OUT

This is the basic law of cause and effect. The Bible emphasizes that you reap what you sow. If you want to make big things happen, you have to take big-time ACTION. Your action plan is so important because it is your playbook to turn your dreams into reality.

Here's the deal…it's this simple. The first step is to determine specifically what it is that you want. The next step is to make a list of what you need to do. If your list doesn't scare you or make you the least bit uncomfortable, it's time to make a new list. Having a goal that feels attainable but slightly out of reach provides focus and direction. The key is to make a range of tasks starting with something you can do today and gradually growing into something that challenges your comfort zone. You have to push yourself to a place that makes you feel uncomfortable—that's the only way you'll grow and improve to levels where you actually reach or exceed your goal.

A powerful inertia is created once you start checking tasks off of your list. It creates a momentum and a confidence that will carry you through the process of achieving your goals. Don't limit yourself with this exercise. Write down what you need to do to reach your goal. Write down as many things as possible, and then get started!

Billionaire investor, Warren Buffett, echoed many before him in warning "The chains of habit are too light to be felt until they are too heavy to be broken." Procrastination is like that; it creeps up on you. Break your old cycle. Create a plan, and take action!

Whether it is making more sales calls per day, seeking a new mentor, joining a gym, learning a new skill, going back to school, asking your crush out on a date, seeking forgiveness, or releasing shame and taking the steps to forgive yourself, whatever you do, you cannot create change while remaining stagnant.

IDENTIFY YOUR WHY

If your reason isn't strong enough, you will not follow through with your goal. Think about a time in your life when you reached a tipping point and you said, "ENOUGH!" You developed enough reasons to get out of that relationship, lose the weight, change careers, or simply choose happiness. What it boils down to is focusing on the pain or pleasure of doing or not doing. Get out of your current situation, and start doing what you love to do. Improve your finances and buy that house. Lose the weight and find energy you never knew existed. Quit those addictive behaviors and renew your relationships. Go back to school and get the education you need to pursue your passion. You will never regret living in your WHY.

Try this: write down the pain and regret you will feel if you don't do what you know you need to do. What will happen if you do not take action? Let these emotions resonate with you; they are strong motivating factors, as well. It's all about having WHY-Power.

Like I mentioned earlier, we all have an internal story we tell ourselves. Usually this story is what drives our actions. I am here to tell you that you are chosen. You are worthy and perfect in your own unique way. Begin to expect amazing things for yourself. Challenge yourself to focus, not just on your goals but on what happiness, joy, satisfaction, and freedom reaching them will create for you and those you love. Having a clear WHY is what's going to move you when you don't feel like moving. If you have a strong enough reason, you can and will do anything.

My WHY-Power is to help as many people I can to have the breakthrough that I encountered in my life. This motivation fuels me to get up early, read, study, listen to audio books and podcasts, learn from mentors, and not waste a single day. My WHY-Power is what is driving me right now as I write this book! It's time you tap into this endless stream of energy. Find your reason. Discover your WHY.

When you master this system, your GPS—*Goal Performance System*—you will set yourself on a course that will take you to your desired destination. Every G4 is equipped with a specialized GPS to take you there. Now it's time to get specific and lock in your coordinates. Set your sights high for a bright future and better tomorrow. The next several chapters will help you determine your where (goal), your how (actions and habits), and your why (reasons). Buckle your seatbelt…it's going to be an amazing ride.

RISE REVIEW

Operate with an internal GPS: Goal Performance System. Identifying a clear goal will be your tracking system and coordinates to take you to your desired destination. The elements that make up the GOALS V acronym will help get you there: gratitude, objective, affirmation, learn, service, and visualization. Enhance your goal setting process by operating in a G4.

THE BIG 4 OF GOAL SETTING (THE G4):
1. Create a GOAL
2. Commit it to PAPER
3. Develop and execute an action PLAN
4. Identify your WHY

Remember to have patience and persistence to see your intention all the way through. This system will set in motion the necessary vision, actions, and mindset to make your goals a reality.

PROJECT RISE

CHAPTER 4
CLEAR VISION = POWER

IF PEOPLE ARE NOT LAUGHING AT YOUR GOALS,
YOUR GOALS ARE TOO SMALL.
-WILLY MERDIANSYAH

This chapter is all about clearly identifying what it is that you want and writing it down with crystal clear clarity. My hope is that you look at this as a challenge to think BIG.

For some of you reading this, it might be hard to comprehend, but it really is true: you CAN accomplish anything you want in life. For some reason, being average and just getting by, is a life that many people live. It may have been modeled in their upbringing. This mindset may have been formed by their socioeconomic level. It could be that people close to you are living with the belief that success only comes to people who get lucky or were born with a silver spoon. Maybe you are one of the people who has tried not once but several times to achieve your dream but have failed multiple times and have finally given up.

I believe that individuals who have extreme wealth in their relationships, finances, and faith have three key traits: DRIVE, KNOWLEDGE, and the ABILITY TO EXECUTE. Recharge your engine and fire up that drive inside of you. Let this book and journaling system be the resource that gives you the knowledge you need and the tools necessary to execute. It is time to roll up your sleeves and go to work.

THE POWER OF WRITING

According to goal-setting expert Brian Tracy, when you write your goals and action plan down on paper, something magical happens. Just simply writing these things down on paper creates what is called a "psycho-neuro motor activity." He adds in his book *No Excuses! The Power of Self-Discipline,* "The act of writing forces you to think and concentrate. It forces you to choose what is more important to you and your future. As a result, when you write down a goal, you impress it into your subconscious mind, which then goes to work twenty-four hours a day to bring your goal to reality." Your subconscious mind is more powerful than your conscious mind. Let it go to work for you. Think about your goals and write them down!

In 2006, *USA Today* reported a study in which researchers divided a large number of people who made New Year's resolutions into two groups: those who wrote their resolutions down and those who didn't. Of the people who set New Year's resolutions, but did not write them down, only 4% actually accomplished their goal. Conversely, the group that wrote down their New Year's resolutions, 44% followed through with their goal. What a huge difference one simple exercise makes! As this illustrates, it's imperative to write down your goals.

The first time I experienced this goal setting phenomenon was when I was 18 years old. I was about to begin my final year of high school football and knew I wanted to accomplish certain achievements before I left for college. One night in my room, I decided to write my goals down on a sheet of paper. No one had taught me this or told me to take this step. For some reason, I just did this on my own. Because I was a wide receiver, I wrote down how many catches and yards receiving I would strive for in each game and for the season. I wrote down that I wanted our team to go to the state playoffs. I also jotted down that I wanted to be All-State and earn a scholarship to play at the Division-I level—that was my REASON—to earn a scholarship that would allow me to experience

54

playing at the highest collegiate level and not worry about paying tuition or room and board.

I put this list above my closet and looked at it every morning before I went to school. So what happened that year? You may have guessed it; our team and I achieved all of the goals I wrote down on that little sheet of paper. I led the league in receiving, I was selected as an All-State Wide Receiver, I earned a full-ride scholarship to Washington State University (Go Cougs!), and even though we lost many great players the year before, we went deep into the state playoffs. Powerful stuff, right?

After this experience, you would think that I would make this process a regular routine. Not yet. For one reason or another, I stopped setting goals and writing them down consistently. I didn't return to it until several years ago when I studied the power of goal setting and learned that most successful people can clearly articulate what it is they want and have created some system to document and achieve their goals.

SEE IT, BE IT

I can still hear my mom cheering for me while up at the plate in a baseball game. While I stood in the batter's box, she'd often yell in encouragement, "See it, be it!" Gosh, aren't moms the best? She knew if I could see my perfect pitch before it came, I would have a much better chance at hitting MY pitch, not the pitcher's pitch. Seeing and believing the outcome before it happens sets the stage for greatness.

Before becoming the youngest champion in the history of the Ultimate Fighting Championship (UFC), Jon Jones would consistently sign his name in an autograph as: "Jon Jones, Champ 2011." The act of thinking about his goal, writing it down, and believing it with all his heart, made all the difference for him to achieve his dream. Jon Jones has now hit some challenging times in his career—maybe it's time he revisits his goals.

Using the "see it, be it" concept my mom instilled in me, I have made writing down my goals a strategic advantage. In using this process, I don't just think about my goals or simply feel them; I can SEE them. The results of making this a ritual has paid off tremendously—from acquiring the income I set out to earn to receiving accolades and rankings in my sales position to fulfilling personal achievements I've striven for—goal setting has changed my life, and I hope you see the value of writing down your goals as a critical strategy as well.

DREAM BIG

Think back to when you were a child. You probably had outrageous goals that would be considered completely unrealistic to your present self. What happened to that child? Where did that hope and optimism go? When did you become "realistic"? Benjamin Franklin was known to have said, "Some people die at 25 and aren't buried until 75."

I remember that I used to dream of being a professional football player and an artist. I used to love to play junior football for the Puyallup Roughriders. At the same time, I had a deep passion for drawing. I was always drawing. It didn't matter what the object was—shoes, trees, animals—pretty much everything was fair game. I even used to make homemade comic books about a house cat that looked very similar to Garfield (I called him "Freaky the Cat").

I have realized in developing my blog *Project Rise*, I am an artist, but in a different form. But my dream of playing professional football started to diminish once I got to junior high and high school. My internal story of being a pro football player definitely stopped in college. I never believed I had what it took to play in the NFL, and guess what happened? My career on the gridiron was finished in Pasadena, California after my last game at the Rose Bowl versus Oklahoma. I guess I was being "realistic."

Here's my hope for you:

STOP BEING REALISTIC, AND DREAM BIG!

Will Smith once said, "Being realistic is the most common path to mediocrity." Break down those old walls that you've built mentally and know that the only limit you have is your mind. Napoleon Hill's top selling book *Think and Grow Rich* teaches us that, "Whatever the brain can conceive and believe it can achieve." So, set unrealistic goals, but with a realistic action plan—that is the key. Just know that the first step is usually the hardest one, but you can do it.

Set benchmark action goals that continually get bigger and more challenging. That is how you build CONFIDENCE and the stamina to keep going. This approach of winning each day over time will be the proven strategy to take you where you want to go.

It's important to set achievable daily goals, but I hope that you do not limit yourself on what you can achieve in the future. Apply this mindset now to create goals in four different time frames:

• Daily
• Monthly
• Annually or Semiannually
• Long-term (three to 10 years)

What happens when we write down clear purposeful goals accompanied by an action plan to achieve them? Whoa baby, look out! There is no stopping you. This is your map that will take you to your buried treasure. Take some time to think about what is it that you want. What do you desire? Make a list, and do not limit yourself. There is no goal too small or too big. After you have spent time making this list, the next step is to narrow your goals to roughly a one month time frame, one year, and one long-term goal that is three to 10 years out. We'll get to your daily goals and objectives a little bit later in Chapter 10.

When you are writing your goals, write them down in a way that describes them as if you already have them. This is a trick I learned from one of the best sales trainers in the world and bestselling author Grant Cardone (check out his book, *The 10X Rule*. It's one of my favorites). Here's an example:

57

I am a New York Times bestselling author.

I am the proud owner of a new home.

I weigh 135 pounds.

Author and positive mindset pioneer Napoleon Hill once said,

GOALS ARE DREAMS WITH A DEADLINE.

I've helped you create a time frame on when you want to achieve your goals (daily, monthly, six months to a year, and long-term). Now it's time to put them to paper.

PERSPECTIVE

Please note that there are times we all fall short and do not hit our goals. That is OK! It's really about the journey and the GROWTH. If you don't achieve your goal, reset, regroup, and re-evaluate what it is that you want. Then revisit your action plan. Remember to have a growth mindset, focusing on PROGRESS, not PERFECTION.

I recently read an article by Paul J. Zak entitled "The Neuroscience of Trust," from the *Harvard Business Review.* He reported that Harvard Business School professor Teresa Amabile found strong data on the power of progress. When Amabile analyzed 12,000 diary entries of employees from a variety of industries, she found that 76% of people reported that their best days involved making progress toward goals.

When you have a narrow and clear target, sometimes you'll miss, but you'll miss small. Imagine how far you'd be off if you didn't create a goal or target. Often times we fail early. That is OK. These experiences are necessary during the process. Consider early missteps as "failing forward." This act is much better than taking no action at all.

To gain perspective, take time right now to think about what it is that you want. This exercise is critical for achieving happiness and being the best version of you. Be as specific as you can. You can do it! Invest in yourself right now. The world is your canvas... consider the masterpiece you want to create, and take the next step by putting that image and outcome to paper.

Here are a few areas to consider when creating your goals: Health, Wealth, Spirituality, Career, Relationships, Volunteering, and Legacy.

I have created a system incorporating many of the areas listed above to help you pinpoint what areas you need to focus on the most to help you RISE. I call this the **7 F's of Fulfillment.**

FAITH: How's your soul? Are you connecting and contributing to something bigger than you?

FAMILY: How are your relationships within your family and significant other?

FRIENDS: How connected are you with those around you? How deep are your friendships right now?

FITNESS: How are your health routines? Are you exercising and eating right? How's your energy?

[F]ILANTHROPY: Are you living a life of giving and serving others?

FINANCES: How are things at work? Do you love what you do? Are you earning the kind of money you want? If you are still in school, are you setting yourself up scholastically to create a quality career? You are never too young to get your hustle on. Figure out a creative way to bring value, while increasing your finances as well.

FUN: Do you have fun each day? Are you prioritizing doing activities that make you laugh, smile, give you energy, and fill your bucket?

I want you to do two things here to help you zero in on your goals. First, rate on a scale from 1 to 10 (1 being poor and 10 being awesome) on how you are doing in these seven areas. Second, force rank each category from 1-7 (1 being the best and 7 needing improvement).

7 F'S OF FULFILLMENT
(1 = poor, 5 = average, 10 = awesome)   Force Rank (1-7)

Faith	1	2	3	4	5	6	7	8	9	10	___
Family	1	2	3	4	5	6	7	8	9	10	___
Friends	1	2	3	4	5	6	7	8	9	10	___
Fitness	1	2	3	4	5	6	7	8	9	10	___
[F]ilanthropy	1	2	3	4	5	6	7	8	9	10	___
Finances	1	2	3	4	5	6	7	8	9	10	___
Fun	1	2	3	4	5	6	7	8	9	10	___

According to NFL great, two-time Super Bowl Champion, and MVP Ray Lewis, the number seven is God's number—the number of completion. That is why Lewis picked the number 52, because five plus two adds up to seven. The world was completed in six days and God rested on the seventh day. When you are in tune and properly aligned in these seven areas of your life, you will feel fulfilled, whole, and more complete than ever.

This process will help you focus on the areas that need to be addressed with more attention and focus. Often times, when we create a better habit to improve a specific area of need, many other parts of our life will follow. This is called a "keystone" habit, which creates a chain reaction of good all around you. For example, when you improve your fitness, often you have more energy to give to your spouse, children, and friends. When you workout regularly, you become mentally refreshed. When you have a clear mind and increased energy, you are more productive at work or school. When you are more productive, you start giving back more to those around you. When you are crushing it at work and are loving and serving others, your finances and wealth begin to increase. With more income, you now have more freedom to travel, live, give, and do the activities that you find entertaining and fun. See the domino effect here?

VISION

I love Lewis Howes. He is a self-made man. After finishing up an all-American college career on the gridiron and in track and field, and following a short stint playing professionally in the Arena Football League, Lewis created multiple million-dollar online businesses. He penned the *New York Times* bestselling book *School of Greatness* and hosts one of the top podcasts on iTunes. Howes is all about vision. He says that vision is a state of mind and that "you become what you envision yourself being."

In the first chapter of *School of Greatness,* he writes, "Your job is to create a vision that makes you want to jump out of bed in the morning. If it doesn't, go back to bed until you have a bigger dream." I love this.

Let these words motivate you to create vision in the *7 F's of Fulfillment.* I call this your Dream-Life Picture. If you could paint the perfect picture of what your life would look like in these seven key areas, what would you be doing? Who would you be sharing it with? How would you feel? In order to create the life you have always wanted, you need vision. Take a moment and write down how you want your life to look and feel in these seven areas as your BEST SELF.

7 F'S OF FULFILLMENT - DREAM-LIFE PICTURE:

FAITH – What are you connecting to that is bigger than yourself?

_____

FAMILY – What do you want your family dynamics and/or your romantic relationship to look and feel like?

_____

FRIENDS – Who is in your inner-circle? How rewarding is your group of friends?

_____

FITNESS – What is your ideal weight, size, and energy level?

_____

[F]ILANTHROPY – What charities, groups, or volunteer agencies are you giving to? How are you helping others each day?

_____

FINANCES – What do you want your career and monthly income to look like?

_____

FUN – What fills your bucket? What activities do you enjoy that you'd like to incorporate more in your day?

_____

I hope this exercise helps you focus in on the areas of your life needing the most attention. Whatever area that is, do not limit yourself! Write down as many goals as you see fit, but remember to be as specific as you can, and write them—in present tense—as if you have already achieved them. Take a moment to write these goals down now. This list will be your true north and the compass that will set everything in motion. Good luck!

RISE REVIEW

Create a new lens for your future by dreaming big. Tap into the spirit of your younger self, when you were a child with no limits.

Rediscover that spirit and reassess your trajectory. When identifying what areas you'd like to improve, let the 7 F's of Fulfillment be a tool to help you pinpoint one or two areas that need to be addressed to achieve happiness.

Remember to have perspective; it will take time to fully actualize your goals. A key strategy to make it happen is to utilize a system of writing down your goals in a layer of time frames: short, mid-range, and long-term. This system will create a goal framework that will help you build and gain momentum over time. We'll discuss this further in the next chapter.

TAKE TIME TO WRITE DOWN YOUR GOALS IN THESE TIME FRAMES:

By this time next month:

_____

In six months to a year:

_____

For the long-term (three to 10 years from now):

_____

HABIT #2: WRITE DOWN YOUR GOALS AND YOUR PLAN

GOALS ARE GREAT, BUT COMMITMENTS ARE BETTER. CHAPTERS 5, 6, 7, AND 8 ARE DESIGNED TO HELP YOU CREATE A PLAN TO MAKE YOUR GOALS A REALITY. BY WRITING DOWN YOUR PLAN, YOU WILL CREATE A PROCESS THAT WILL HELP YOU DO THE MOST IMPORTANT ACTIVITY TO BE YOUR BEST SELF: TAKE ACTION! THIS SECTION WILL ALSO TAKE YOUR ACTION PLAN TO THE NEXT LEVEL. BY IDENTIFYING THE REASONS BEHIND YOUR GOAL, ESTABLISHING NEW DAILY HABITS, AND MASTERING A SYSTEM OF WRITING YOUR INTENTIONS DOWN, YOU WILL BUILD A MACHINE THAT IS ALL ABOUT EXECUTION AND ACCOUNTABILITY.

CHAPTER 5
ACTIONS BEAT IDEAS

ACTION CONQUERS FEAR.

-PETER NIVIO ZARLENGA

Way to go! Now that you have zeroed in on what you want, it's time to think about what you must DO to turn your goals into reality. Goal achievement is all about taking action. There are two types of goals:

1. Outcome goals
2. Action goals

Which have the most power: outcome goals or action goals? An outcome goal is the end result, whereas an action goal is what it takes to get you there. There is no question—everything starts with an idea and a vision, BUT actions beat ideas. Completing action goals will take you to your desired outcome. It's all about implementation and then getting things done. Social media mogul, advertising guru, entrepreneur extraordinaire, and CEO of VaynerMedia, Gary Vaynercuk, sums it up well: "Ideas are S#%@, execution is the game." Average achievers take average action. High achievers, like Gary V., exert an insane amount of action and activity. Movement, hustle, grinding, motion, activity, and action MUST take place for you to make your goals happen! Take ownership of your thoughts and your actions. Go for it!

I've already mentioned the power of the Law of Attraction, how your thoughts manifest the things in your life (I'll get more into this topic later.). A thought without action is worthless. A dream without execution will not develop. If you harness the power of the Law of Attraction with another universal law, the Law of Cause and Effect, you won't be stopped! According to IQMatrix.com (who specialize in self-growth and mind maps), The Law of Cause and Effect states that for every effect there is a definite cause, likewise for every cause there is a definite effect. Your thoughts, behaviors, and ACTIONS create specific effects that create your life as you know it.

One might say: "I'm afraid to take action because it's risky." "I might get laughed at." "I could fail." "What will others think?"

Trust me, it is just as risky TO AVOID ACTION and remain on the sidelines of life. According to legendary artist Pablo Picasso, "Action is the foundational key to all success." Your outcomes are a direct byproduct and consequence of your actions. Trust me, in order to achieve anything worthwhile in life, you must take DETERMINED ACTION!

PAIN

There is pain in either direction you choose to go. If you do not take action, it is most likely you will feel frustrated that you are not living the life you want. You might feel the pain of not having the physical health you strive for because you haven't establish a disciplined exercise plan. Your career isn't where you think it should be, and you are struggling paycheck to paycheck because you haven't taken the necessary steps to invest in your development and advance your career.

Or there is the pain of working extremely hard. The pain of sacrificing sleep or episodes of your favorite TV shows to work on your craft. Or the pain of telling certain people in your life that you cannot hang out with them anymore because their lifestyle, lack of ambition, or laziness is holding you back.

Whatever your case may be, you must make a plan in order to achieve the life you strive to live. Let me share with you a very personal example of taking action.

There was a time while Kendra and I were dating and decided to take a break—it was Kendra's idea, not mine. Kendra was the first girl in my life that I truly loved, and I was absolutely crushed when she shared her feelings to take time apart. Her decision to breakup was a byproduct of me being very selfish, consumed by juggling multiple sports and hobbies, working many hours, and basically doing whatever I wanted. What can I say? I was young and dumb. She reached a tipping point and needed some space.

The night after she told me she wanted out, I was lucky to have gotten even one hour of sleep. I was balling my eyes out trying to figure out what I was going to do without her. I had finally found "the one" and I thought I had lost her. Luckily, I had a regional work meeting all week in Portland starting the next day. Being surrounded by my close friends and colleagues and staying busy running to different meetings and activities was a huge distraction and blessing. The night I got back home from my meeting, I did something that I want YOU to do. I needed to fill my hurt, loneliness, and sorrow with something positive, so I developed an action plan.

I pulled out a piece of paper from my drawer by my bed and just started writing. I titled the page, "My Off-Season Plan." I knew that this was a season in my life, and that God had something amazing out there for me (This may similar to what you may be going through right now. If so, remember: it's just a season, not forever.). I saw this time like an athlete's off-season—four to seven months to get my mind, body, and spirit ready for another shot at love—whether is was a new relationship or getting back together with Kendra, it would be "a new season." I made a list of the many things I needed to do to better myself. My list looked something like this:
• Channel my energy into a consistent workout plan to improve my fitness
• Workout four days a week
• Play in the winter men's basketball league
• Eat healthier

- ⁻ Cut fast food down to only twice a month
- ⁻ Increase greens and fruit (at least one of each per meal)
- Go to church each week
- Read my Bible daily and do my daily devotions
- Join the men's small group that meets on Thursday mornings
- Have electrolysis done on the hair on my neck and shoulders (sorry if I'm getting too personal!)
- Practice at least one random act of kindness everyday

This list gave me purpose. This action plan gave me direction. By taking time to create my offseason game plan, I was able to turn my sorrow into excitement. I used that time to focus on myself, which would get me ready for my next shot at a relationship...but I wasn't done.

I also created what I called, "The Blueprint" for how I was going to carry myself and treat my future wife. I listed 20 actions on how I was going to treat my bride, numerically prioritized in order of importance. These two documents fueled massive action in my life, and I was able to bounce back and become a better person because of this hardship. I am so proud to say that Kendra and I got back together four months after we broke up. On December 4, 2009, I framed "The Blueprint" and gave it to Kendra just before I proposed to her. We have been happily married for over seven years now, and I owe most of my growth and joy to that original action list that I created when we first broke up. Today she has "The Blueprint" framed in her office.

My action plan turned this negative experience and pain into the single most positive force and joy in my life—my relationship with my favorite person in the world: my tall, sexy, smart, hysterical, talented, amazing wife, the mother of my children, Kendra.

OK, enough about me, now back to you. It's time for you to make your list. While making your own "Blueprint," I'd like you to rethink a saying you have already been exposed to before. You may have heard the phrase "quality over quantity." Well, I'd like you to switch these around when striving to reach your action goals.

70

Think "quantity over quality." Do not let perfect get in the way of good. Perfection and fear of failure are the enemies of creativity while repetition is the mother of mastery. The more you do whatever it is you want to accomplish, the better you will become. Start small, and slowly build with each task on your action plan. This undoubtedly will instill the confidence you'll need to keep going and to stay on track.

MAKE IT MEASURABLE

In order to make the most out of your action plan, you need to decide when, where, or how often you will perform that task in advance. In other words, once you have written down your action step, add a date, time, and frequency. When will you execute this step? How frequently? An example of this concept would look like this: "On Monday, Wednesday, and Friday, I will go to the gym for an hour before I go to work."

According to Heidi Grant Halvorson PhD, social psychologist, speaker, associate director of Columbia Business School's Motivation Science Center, and author of *9 Things Successful People Do Differently*, "Studies show that this kind of planning will help your brain to detect and seize the opportunity when it arises, increasing your chances of success by roughly 300 percent." Grant Halvorson calls this strategy *if-then* planning. *If-then* plans refer to:
If X happens (date, time, event), then I will do Y (activity or action item).

Dr. Halvorson noted in her lecture that I attended that over 100 studies have shown that this approach can double or triple your chances of success! For example, in one study looking at sticking with a consistent exercising routine, 91 percent of if-then planners were still exercising regularly weeks later versus 39 percent of non-planners. The evidence is clear—the more specific you can be with your action plan, the more successful you will be at executing it.

71

GOAL HIERARCHY

When you are operating with a goal framework or hierarchy, you will unify your goals to serve one purpose and overarching vision. This approach keeps you on track and motivated during challenging times and setbacks. Your action steps will serve you by creating lower-level goals that funnel up to mid-level and big goals. This process is most impactful when all levels are aligned. Take a look at the diagram below.

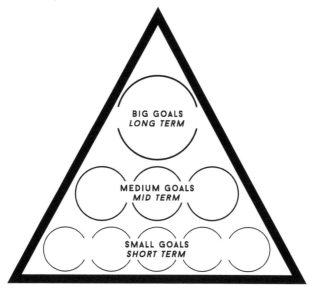

GOAL HIERARCHY

There are three levels to the Goal Hierarchy: small or short-term goals, medium or mid-term goals, and big goals or long-term goals. Because there is no such thing as overnight success, this system and mindset will help you sustain your vision and give you the characteristics necessary to make your goal a reality as you develop perseverance and patience along the way. A perfect example of operating in this framework is the story of the 2016 World Series

Champions, the Chicago Cubs.

As General Manager of the Boston Red Sox for nine years, Theo Epstein guided this franchise to two World Series championships after being shut out for 86 years. This Yale University graduate, who also has a law degree, was called the "Boy Genius" by leading the Sox to their first title before he turned 30 years old.

In 2011, Epstein took his talents to Chicago as President of Baseball Operations in hopes of bringing a championship to another storied franchise who hadn't won a World Series since 1908—the Cubs. Many insiders and friends told him that this move was career suicide, but Epstein had a vision and a plan—and this plan, if done right, would take time but bring results.

Once in Chicago, fans would stop Epstein in the streets and ask him, "When are our beloved Cubbies going to win a World Series?" He would usually smile and tell the adoring fan, "It will happen, but you'll have to wait a few years." Epstein knew the product he wanted to produce, but understood it wouldn't happen overnight.

Many changes and action steps needed to take place in order to reach the ultimate goal of reversing the curse and bringing home a world title to the Windy City. What the Cubs achieved occurred in multiple steps over time. Here's what Epstein set out to do:

• Revamp the scouting personnel and department
• Change how they scouted players—scout the person, not just the player
• Build a solid foundation of talent through the MLB draft, not just by acquiring free agents (e.g. 2013 first-round draft pick and all-star third baseman Kris Bryant)
• Change the culture within the entire organization to be all about effort and attitude
• Improve the facilities within the organization
• Hire a manager who will carry out the values instilled by Epstein and lead through "The Cub Way" (In 2014, the Cubs found the right fit in former Tampa Bay Rays manager, Joe Maddon.)
• Win the division

- Win the pennant
- Win the World Series

The 2016 World Series Champion Chicago Cubs can teach us that it starts by having a vision and a plan, then executing that plan to accomplish the vision. True success occurs when your goals and action steps are operating within a goal hierarchy system—with passion, perseverance, and patience. You too can turn what once was thought impossible to possible, just like Epstein and the Cubs. It starts by developing the staying power and the patience to see it through.

NOW IT'S YOUR TURN

It's time to create your plan! Once your list is complete, go back and prioritize your list in numeric order and create an *if-then* plan. Focus on your most important action items first. Once a task is complete, check it off and begin to feel your confidence, pride, and momentum build. Build up what I call your M&M—Mental Momentum. Momentum is a powerful force. Use this to your advantage and go get what it is you want!

Here is an example of a goal and action plan that hits close to home for me:

GOAL
I am an effective and competent communicator who can present with passion, speak with confidence, and read aloud with authority in any environment or in front of any audience. In my field, I am the most sought-after speaker in Washington State and top 10 in the country.

ACTIONS (Notice there is a date or frequency per action item—this is KEY!)
1. Talk to my mentor about my lack of self-confidence in speaking in public settings. I will schedule this meeting by September 15, and they will help me

74

come up with a plan to improve my fluency.
2. Enroll in speech therapy by October 1.
3. Join a Toastmasters Club to practice public speaking by December 1—attend meetings once per week.
4. Complete 10 speeches at Toastmasters and earn my Competent Communicator Certificate.
5. Take an improv-comedy class for at least three months.
6. Volunteer to present at as many work meetings as possible (goal: one talk per quarter).
7. Volunteer to speak at a minimum of one community event per month (church, schools, athletics, etc.).
8. Secure three paid speaking gigs a month by June 1.
9. Become a sought-after speaker who is financially compensated for giving speeches and talks (by 2020, I will be earning 50% of my income from paid speeches).

Do you see how my action plan is in numeric order and progresses to more challenging tasks over time? Also, did you notice there is date or frequency measure included as well? Both are crucial to making your goals and action plan become actualized.

Just to give you an update on my progress, I'm executing step eight on my list right now and I'm working toward number nine!

The most challenging step is the first one, but if you put time and energy into this critical step of writing down what actions you MUST do, not SHOULD do (Many people, "should" all over themselves.), you'll set in motion the momentum needed to see your plan all the way through. There is a definite possibly that new ideas will come to you throughout your journey. Your action plan is a living and breathing document. Add to this list as you go. Start small and build. Reaching your ultimate goals will take time. Do not get discouraged. A way to prevent this is to think of your action plan like a flight of stairs—you rise with each step.

Goal guru Brian Tracy suggests listing 20 action items. Once you get past number ten, Tracy suggests, you come up with your best ideas.

As you write your list, don't worry about putting them in sequential order at first—simply write down all the things you need to do. Once you have listed all of the steps you can think of, go back and force rank each of these action steps in order of when it is realistically achievable. Starting with the smallest and most important action item as number "1," move down the list and identify numbers 2, 3, and so on. This technique will help you create your plan. Once you have finished ranking each action, add the date or time frame by which you'd like to accomplish the task or note how frequently you'd like to perform the task.

Over time, you'll look back and think, "Wow, look how far I've come." Just practice the patience and the wisdom to understand that it will never be perfect. Your success will not happen overnight; it might take years. That's the pitfall of many—they give their action plan a week, month, or even a year and quit just before a breakthrough. Don't let this be you! Invest and be prepared to fight for the long haul.

Clarity is power. Hone in on what actions you must take and take them. This is the only way to achieve greatness: through effort, hard work, and action.

RISE REVIEW

There are two types of goals: action goals and outcome goals. Without question, action goals are more powerful—focus on the action, not the outcome. An idea without execution is worthless.

Include an "if-then" plan to improve the likelihood of following through with your action steps and remember to have patience.

Creating your goals and action steps within a goal hierarchy will help you stay on task for the long haul. Remember it's all about quantity not quality as you get started. The more you do, the better you'll get, and the more momentum you'll create.

Here are the steps to create your action plan:

MAKE A LIST: Make a list of all the actions necessary to achieve your goal. Don't worry about the order.

PRIORITIZE: Review your list and force rank (prioritize) each action step in numeric fashion (1, 2, 3, etc.).

MAKE IT MEASURABLE: For each action step, include a date, time, or frequency. This will increase your likelihood—by roughly 300 percent—of making it happen.

Now it's your turn to create your ACTION PLAN.

_____

_____

_____

_____

_____

_____

_____

_____

_____

77

CHAPTER 6
JUST GIVE ME A REASON

I SURVIVED BECAUSE THE FIRE INSIDE OF ME BURNED BRIGHTER
THAN THE FIRE AROUND ME.
-JOSHUA GRAHAM

Awesome work! You are now well on your way to creating a rock-solid plan to RISE. Look at the goals and action steps you just created. Now think about WHY you want to make these accomplishments a reality. Here's the deal, reasons resonate. People buy feelings not facts. If there is no feeling or emotion connected to your vision, you will not act or follow through. In this stage, you need to come up with reasons that represent your WHY-Power.

There are two main types of motivators: extrinsic and intrinsic. Think of extrinsic motivators as things (e.g. a car, a house, expensive clothes, or other material possessions). Conversely, think of intrinsic motivators as feelings or states of being (e.g. freedom, peace of mind, safety, or security). If someone is using only extrinsic motivation to drive themselves, they might not be able to sustain the happiness they are after. The new car or expensive pair of shoes will only make you feel on cloud nine for a limited time before you are searching for something else.

Harnessing the power of intrinsic motivation and seeking fulfillment from internal sources is where the magic happens. My intrinsic motivation to write, speak, mentor, and inspire others is to one day create a lifestyle where I am in total control of what I do and to help others do the same. My goal is to earn enough income by doing what I love—utilizing *Project Rise* as a conduit to help and to serve others—so Kendra doesn't have to work if she doesn't want to. That piece of mind, freedom, and joy of taking control of my destiny to support my family is what drives me.

WHAT DRIVES YOU AND PUSHES YOU FORWARD?

Here's an example of how finding your "why," and tying an extrinsic motivator with an intrinsic one makes all the difference:

In the 1930s and 1940s, Byron Nelson was one of the best golfers on the PGA Tour and in the world. He was a true talent and had a passion for the game, yet his ultimate dream was to be a rancher. One day, the Texas native was out on a drive with his wife, Louise, and came across a beautiful ranch. This stunning property had everything Nelson was looking for: land, animals, and the perfect ranch-style home. Feeling inspired and bold, they drove up to the property and asked the owner how much it would take to buy the property. The owner politely said that it wasn't for sale. Not letting this shake him, Nelson kindly asked the gentleman again to just give him a number. He asked, "What would it take for you to sell?"

The rancher thought about it for a moment, wrote the number down, and gave it to Nelson. With a clear goal in his mind and a powerful motivator, Nelson embarked on his last full season on the PGA tour. What happened that year had never been achieved before nor has ever been seen again. His reason, or WHY-Power, to see his dream fulfilled created a drive and a purpose that manifested a year for the ages. That 1945 season, Nelson won an eye-popping 11 tournaments in a row and an astonishing 18 tournaments during that year. Both records still hold to this day.

When the season was over, a reporter asked Nelson, "How did you do it?" He explained that it was simple; he knew how much money in cash he needed to buy his dream ranch, so he went out and earned it. He told the reporters that whenever he drilled a birdie putt, he would say, "That's another cow for Louise!"

Nelson retired the next year, and he and his wife became ranchers. The power of WHY is real.

PROSOCIAL MOTIVATION

When you tie intrinsic motivation with a concept called prosocial motivation, you'll create even more WHY-Power. With prosocial motivation, you are motivated by the need to help others. This form of motivation is the strongest form of motivation. It's no longer about you, but rather about the people you care about and how your actions affect them.

While traveling in Argentina in 2006, entrepreneur Blake Mycoskie noticed that hundreds of children were running around without any shoes on their feet. This hardship really impacted him. What he did next was revolutionary. He created a for-profit organization that donates one pair of shoes to children in need for every one pair sold. You may have heard of this company, TOMS. Their prosocial motivation is the motto: "One for one." For every shoe they sell, they give one to a child in need. This giving model has evolved into more than just shoes.

TOMS has not only provided over 60 million shoes to children since 2006, but TOMS Eyewear has restored sight to over 400,000 since 2011; TOMS Roasting Company has helped provide over 335,000 weeks of safe water since 2014; and in 2015, TOMS Bag Collection provided safe birth services for over 25,000 mothers.

Like TED talk superstar, author, and leadership expert Simon Sinek's book *Start With Why* suggests, people buy why you do what you do, not what or how you do it. In nurturing an intrinsic desire tied into a prosocial motivator, as in the TOMS example, you will find that you are the not only one acting on your vision. You'll be surrounded by others inspired by your WHY-Power.

THREE CHALLENGES

Byron Nelson's and Blake Mycoskie's stories illustrate that strong reasons fuel intentions, mindset, and actions. However,

there are three obstacles that everyone faces when seeking to improve and achieve their goals. I call this FAT. If you want to live a "FAT life" and live the life of your dreams, you need to overcome:
1. Feelings
2. Adversity
3. Time

Feelings + Adversity + Time = FAT. Looking at these with the wrong perspective results in a "FAT chance" you'll meet your goals (ok, I'm done with the FAT analogies, I promise) .

FEELINGS

When faced with a task, many people say, "Oh, I'll start next week," or, "Once my ducks are in a row, I'll begin." Or they don't take action because of these five dreadful words: *I don't feel like it.* For example, 6:00 a.m. Monday morning is going to come, and you are not going to FEEL like moving. Making necessary sacrifices aren't easy. Procrastination and waiting on feelings alone won't help you get the job done. You need to DECIDE to take action and, like the Nike slogan, "Just Do It."

Do not let your environment decide your attitude. If you allow your circumstance to dictate whether you take action or not, or worse yet, to formulate your attitude, you will not go very far. You create your attitude when you COMMIT to take action, not just when it feels convenient. High achievers understand this. They have the willpower, to NOT focus on the pain of taking action, but to HONE IN on the gain that the end result will generate. They will continue to generate as they put in the work. No one ever says, "Man I wish I didn't work out, or "I shouldn't have read a book that improved my personal develop (while they binged for five hours on Netflix)." Overcome your lower nature and you will build a fantastic future. How do you do that? By having WHY-Power!

To illustrate this, let's examine working out (one of my favorite pastimes). If you focus your attention and energy on the not-so-exciting thought of getting up early, running on the treadmill, and the

82

pain of lifting weights—you won't move. Instead, focus all of your energy on how you will feel when you get going and into the zone midway through. Focus on how awesome you will feel when your workout is complete. You'll feel a sense of completion, less stress, mental clarity, and you'll have more energy to attack the day.

When feelings and thoughts pop into your mind, tempting you to hit the metaphorical snooze button, run through all of the remarkable benefits you will feel when your task is complete, rather than ruminating on the few things that you don't enjoy at the outset. Just take that first step and your momentum will build, and you'll be well on your way. If you do the thing that you used to put off with enough frequency, you'll create a new habit loop and new craving (the positive feeling that working out creates). Then, the thought of NOT DOING the task will become more painful than actually doing it.

Don't be like the many people out there who love sleeping, looking at Instagram, or playing video games more than achievement. Focus on the gain of the outcome instead of the pain of getting started. This feat is easier to execute when you harness your WHY-Power.

ADVERSITY

The time in your life when you won't have problems is the day you are dead (What did Biggie say? "More money, more problems."). I don't care who you are, how much money you make, or where you live, WE ALL HAVE PROBLEMS. WE ALL FACE ADVERSITY. You'll fail not once, not twice, not three times, but many times over. The difference between winners and losers is that winners have a strong enough WHY-Power to avoid stopping when disappointment hits. During your journey there will be setbacks: you might lose funding, it might be a horrible time in the marketplace, or someone in your crew will mess up or intentionally screw you over. Your WHY is the only thing that will keep you fighting through adversity.

83

Generally, the most successful people in life have failed the most—but they have a crucial personality trait called grit. Grit and persistence are often the deciding factor in one hitting or missing their end goal. The difference between these individuals and those who quit all comes down to their WHY-Power.

Our culture is rich with examples of people who fail forward. Here are a few of my favorites:

• **Walt Disney** was turned down 302 times before finally getting financing to build his Disney dynasty.

• Twelve publishers turned down **J.K. Rowlings'** manuscript for *Harry Potter*.

• Before winning multiple NBA MVP awards, Golden State's **Steph Curry** didn't even make the all-star team until his fifth season (Before going to the NBA, he wasn't even offered a college scholarship from a major conference university.).

Abraham Lincoln lost seven political elections before being elected president in 1860.

At the age of 65, unsatisfied with his $105 social security check, **Colonel Sanders** shopped his fried chicken recipe around and was turned down as astonishing 1,009 times before founding Kentucky Fried Chicken.

The moral of the story is: keep fighting and keep going. Build and learn from your failure. Never quit! One of the first quotes my father had me memorize might be the most impactful. It's from the great Dr. Martin Luther King, Jr.: "The ultimate measure of a man is not where he stands in moments of comfort and convenience, but where he stands in times of challenge and controversy."

YOUR REASON AND MOTIVES WILL BE THE FIRE THAT PUSHES YOU FORWARD, INSTEAD OF CONSUMING YOU AND HOLDING YOU BACK.

TIME

Here's what I call the *Champion's Challenge:* who can sustain the highest level of focus, commitment, intensity, and drive for the longest period of time? Anyone can grind and go hard for one day, one week, one month, or even for one year. Champions and the best of the best can sustain the energy, action, and activity it requires for a long as it takes to make their dreams happen.

While speaking in front of a large audience, entrepreneur and motivational speaker Les Brown asked his audience, "It ain't over until…" He then paused, and the audience fell into his trap, yelling, "It's OVER!" He smiled and said, "No! It ain't over until I WIN!"

Do not stop. Keep pushing toward your goal. If you can sustain that Beast Mode mentality over time, I promise BIG THINGS will come. Having strong and clear WHY-Power will help give you that patience and persistence needed to take you to the top.

Take it from author and professor Angela Duckworth's breakthrough book *Grit: The Power of Passion and Persistence*, "Consistency of effort in the long haul is everything."

T. ROB

My favorite life strategist and performance coach, Tony Robbins, has a clear WHY, which has been evident throughout his nearly 40 years in the personal development industry. The reason he is a repeat *New York Times* bestselling author, has fed millions of people around the world through his foundation, has coached presidents, CEOs, professional athletes, and leaders reach their potential is that he doesn't want people to hurt like he did as a child and a teen.

Tony Robbins grew up poor with an absent father and an abusive mother. Even meals weren't a guarantee. One Thanksgiving, his family did not have food to eat to celebrate the holiday. What happened that night changed his life: a stranger delivered a turkey dinner for his family to enjoy. This single act of generosity and kindness spawned Robbins' desire to give back to others as well.

Instead of being a victim, Robbins channeled that energy and pain of scarcity into something positive. He used his pain to create his WHY. He also channeled the joy he felt on the receiving end of a random act of kindness. The elation that he felt when someone helped him created the need and the WHY to do the same for others.

Now equipped with a WHY, Robbins began an obsessive journey to understand success and share that knowledge with others to help end the suffering of as many people as possible. He invested in his developing his knowledge and skill to help others. To improve his efficiency, he took a speed reading class and learned to absorb dozens of books each month. Later, he was mentored by the great self-help pioneer Jim Rohn. Robbins' WHY-Power has made all the difference, and he uses it daily to motivate himself to help people and change lives all over the world.

Like Robbins and other successful people, having a clear WHY is what drives their purpose, their philanthropy, and their profits. You got WHY-Power? The stronger your WHY-Power, the more successful you'll become, and your ability to lead and inspire others will be magnetic for years, not just seasons.

Reflect: what memories, desires, ambitions, and passions can you identify that will fuel your motives and actions?

DRIVE VS. PRESS

Peter Bregman is an advisor to CEOs from big companies and startups. He specializes in leadership and improving today's work life and is the author of the book *18 Minutes*. He gives great advice that ties into having a clear REASON. He says, "You need to accept that you can't do everything. Then you need to make sure that the goals you have are really yours." When you have a clear goal and a WHY, this creates DRIVE and success. However, when your WHY is in the wrong place, you will PRESS and not sustain the level of greatness you are seeking.

When your WHY is misguided, you feel the need to PRESS to achieve your goal.

PRESS

P – Pressure
Unhealthy pressure increases unwanted anxiety
R – Retaliation
If your WHY is to seek revenge, your success will be short-lived
E – Expectation of others
This motivation leads to a path of hollowness and un-fulfillment
S – Someone else's goal
It's hard to sustain a high level of passion when it's not your goal
S – Stuck
Lack of control creates stress, which limits performance

If your motivation falls into one of the examples listed above, it's time to revisit your path, vision, and WHY. Below are examples of what you will create when your goals, actions, and reasons are aligned. You create the inner DRIVE needed to overcome moments when you "don't feel like it" or are faced with adversity. This mindset will give you the willpower necessary to stay committed for the long haul.

DRIVE

D – Discipline
A clear WHY gives you the power to build strong sustaining habits
R – Resilience
If you have a compelling reason to get up when you fail, you will
I – Inspiration
A healthy motivation breeds inspiration, which spawns action
V – Value
A deep and passionate reason will spill over to all who are around you
E – Energy
When your WHY is your own, it generates enthusiasm and excitement

REVISIT

Throughout your journey and quest to achieve your goals, reference back to this list of WHY you are putting forth all your effort. Let these reasons fuel your actions and re-motivate you during seasons of challenge, adversity, and hardship. Trust me, the question isn't IF, it's WHEN will challenges come. This list will serve as your charger—similar to the charger you use for your cell phone—it will give you the POWER to function and keep going. Your REASONS and your WHY will invigorate your soul as you resolve to attack each day with excitement and purpose. Let's go! Bring it, world! I have my WHY, thus I have my super power!

And now, here is the REASON behind the personal GOAL I discussed in the previous chapter.

GOAL

I am an effective and competent communicator who can present with passion, speak with confidence, and read out loud with authority in any environment or in front of any audience. In my field, I am the most sought-after speaker in Washington State and top 10 in the country.

REASON

My confidence as a public speaker will be greatly improved; my talent will allow me to speak to audiences that will help improve lives; my ability to acquire impactful and high-paying opportunities will increase; through this growth and contribution to society, I will create a more fulfilled and happy life for myself and others.

Below are more examples of having a REASON for specific GOALS. The reasons, or WHY-Power, are in bold.

I am a New York Times bestselling author. – **I aspire to impact thousands of lives in a positive way through my writing. Because of my struggle and RISE, I yearn to help others who**

88

have gone through or are going through what I had to over-come. My purpose is to help people become the best version of themselves.

I am the proud owner of a new home. – I desire to have the financial freedom to invest and provide a safe and stable environment for family and myself.

I weigh 135 pounds. – I want to be healthier and love the way I look and feel everyday! With a healthier body and more energy, I can be more active and play with my kids without getting tired.

RISE REVIEW

There are several types of motivation that create WHY-Power: extrinsic, intrinsic, and prosocial. Link an intrinsic motivator to your WHY to give yourself the energy and stamina necessary to sustain your trajectory. Also, tie an intrinsic desire with a prosocial motivator, the need to help and impact others. This combination is the most powerful form of motivation.

Be familiar with the three main obstacles that stand in the way of achieving your goals, including: 1) Feelings, 2) Adversity, and 3) Time. When faced with these challenges, focus on the gain not the pain when deciding whether or not to take action.

Understand that failure is part of the growth process. The best of the best understand this and learn from their failures instead of letting those setbacks define them. Failure is a building block to success, not a roadblock.

Remember to make sure your reasons are in the right place. Seeking a target that isn't truly yours because you are feeling PRESSED by someone else is no way to create lasting happiness. Making your reasons your own creates DRIVE to overcome the many challenges that you will face along your journey.

Now it's your turn! List your REASONS for the GOALS you previously listed.

How will these goals feel when achieved? How will they help, serve, and impact others? What will give me WHY-Power?

Reasons For My Goals:

_____

_____

_____

_____

_____

_____

_____

_____

CHAPTER 7
UPGRADE TO A G5

YOU'LL NEVER CHANGE YOUR LIFE UNTIL YOU CHANGE
SOMETHING YOU DO DAILY. THE SECRET OF YOUR SUCCESS
IS FOUND IN YOUR DAILY ROUTINE.
- JOHN C. MAXWELL

Awesome job! You are now ahead of a vast majority of your peers by simply taking these steps in completing the Big 4 of Goal Setting: 1) Creating a clear GOAL, 2) Committing it to PAPER, 3) Developing and executing an ACTION PLAN, and 4) Identifying your WHY. So now it's time to stop dreaming and START DO-ING.

The next step of turning your dreams into reality boils down to one simple concept. It's upgrading your G4 Jet to a G5, a more decked out model that's bigger, faster, and more valuable. I have added one more step to your goal setting and achieving process. This approach is time-tested and will lead you to your deepest plea-sure or your greatest failure. That one thing is your HABITS. It's time to step up to the Big 5 of Goal Setting.

THE BIG 5 OF GOAL SETTING (G5):
1. Create a GOAL
2. Commit it to PAPER
3. Develop and execute an action PLAN
4. Identify your WHY
5. **Upgrade your HABITS**

Take a moment and envision a jet or an airplane. Each of the five elements of successful goal setting (G5) represent a different part of the aircraft.

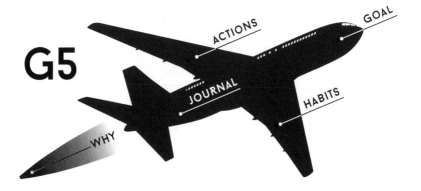

• In front of the jet is your GOAL, where you are headed; it clarifies your direction and ultimate destination.
• The wings represent your ACTIONS and your HABITS, which give you lift and elevate you to your desired achievement.
• The jet propulsion, or back of the plane, represents your WHY; it gives you power and pushes you forward; it's the fuel and energy that makes you go.
• The body of the jet represents your JOURNAL and the power of putting your GOAL and PLAN on PAPER; it will carry you to your destination.

This last addition, in which you upgrade from G4 to G5, is all about mastering your habits. Show me someone who is successful or someone who is constantly struggling and living a life of scarcity, and I'll ask this one question, "How are their habits?" Your happiness and achievements are a byproduct of your standards and what you are willing to tolerate.

One of my favorite quotes, which I often share, is from Aristotle. He wisely said, "We are what we repeatedly do. Excellence is not an act, but a HABIT."

Remember what I said earlier, that in order to be an expert at anything in life, it starts with mastering the fundamentals. Part of mastering the fundamentals is being intentional with your habits and committing to being disciplined. Establishing these patterns and rituals are necessary to create a shift and RISE in your satisfaction and fulfillment. Being mindful of your habits, good or bad, is a vital fundamental you MUST master.

HABIT LOOP

Charles Duhigg is a Pulitzer Prize-nominated investigative reporter who writes for the New York Times. He is the author of *The Power of Habit: Why We Do What We Do in Life and Business.* In this book, Duhigg explains how important habits, from brushing our teeth to smoking to exercising, play an important role in our lives. What's more, he explains exactly how these habits form. He notes that research suggests that as many as 40 percent of the actions we perform each day are based on habit and not on conscious decisions. According to Duhigg, any habit can be broken down into a three-part loop: Cue–Routine–Reward. To complete the cycle, a "craving" is created, which helps continue the cycle.

Can you think of any examples like this in your life? When you wake up, do you drink coffee? When you get home from work, do you tap and swipe away with your smartphone?

When seeking to make a change, it's important to create what Duhigg calls a "keystone habit," which fosters a new routine and often sets off a chain reaction for other positive habits to follow. For example, regular exercise often generates healthier eating patterns. Below are some examples of keystone habits:

• **Planning your days.** This habit helps you zero in on what you need to accomplish, which results in greater productivity.
• **Meditating.** This act reduces anxiety, increases memory, and improves goal achievement.
• **Developing daily routines.** Creating routines impacts our health, productivity, finances, and consistency which produces a cascade of positive outcomes.

- **Exercising regularly.** This habit increases patience and effectiveness at work while reducing stress.
- **Making your bed.** Bed-makers are more likely to own a home, enjoy their job, exercise regularly, and live happier.
- **Tracking what you eat.** Duhigg cites a 2009 study by the *National Institute of Health* in which participants who journaled what they ate lost twice as much weight as those who didn't. This is another example of the power of writing things down.

In 2015, Washington Nationals slugger Bryce Harper won the Major League Baseball Most Valuable Player (MVP) award. However, he didn't start the season off on a strong note. In the month of April, he was barely hitting over .200. He was labeled by Matt Williams, his manager at the time, as a "5 o'clock hero." Meaning, at 5 p.m., while taking batting practice on the field, he would put on a show like no one else in the Major Leagues. His power was a sight to see—he would hit effortless homeruns all over the field. The fans loved it. Yet, this approach created bad habits that carried over into the game and affected his performance. He was over-swinging.

Harper realized this and made one habit change: he stopped taking batting practice out on the field, instead creating a routine in which he practiced in the indoor batting cages, undercover where no one could see him. He developed a disciplined system of working on his fundamentals, a system he was able to execute during game time. This single shift made all the difference. At the completion of the 2015 season, Harper generated the third highest Wins Above Replacement (WAR) score in the history of the MLB. The keystone habit and discipline of taking batting practice inside with no one watching versus entertaining the fans during pregame made all the difference.

Habits can positively affect all walks of life, not just in sports. Duhigg cites a 2005 University of Pennsylvania study that suggests that students with high self-discipline perform better than those with a high IQ: "They had fewer absences and spent less time watching television and more hours on homework." Talent is given. Skill is earned. Great habits beat ability every day of the week. These tools that I share with you in this book will help instill habits that have the potential to be life-changing…but only if you stick to them!

What is a habit that you need to revisit? Make journaling one of your keystone habits that sets into motion more clarity, purpose, and improved daily rituals.

IF-THEN PLAN

Remember in **Chapter 5: Actions Beat Ideas**, I noted the power of if-then plans? This concept is so important, I want to revisit it, and give it more context. Not only did I read Heidi Grant Halvorson's book, *9 Things Successful People Do Differently*, I have also had the pleasure of listening to her lecture live, discussing how to improve mindset and habits. According to her research, the two biggest mistakes in executing one's goals are:

1. Not identifying exactly what we need to do (lacking specific action steps), and

2. Missing an opportunity to act (The statement, "I don't have time" is never true—you have time—you just choose to do something else with your time.).

The key to overcome these pitfalls is to create an *if-then* plan. Grant Halvorson shared that this strategy is the most important finding in 50 years of researching goal achievement. When you have an *if-then* plan, you specify what you will do and when and where you will do it in advance. Here are a few examples:

• If I have not already done so, once it hits 4 p.m. on Fridays, I will complete and turn in my expense report.

• On Monday morning, I will take 10 minutes to prioritize my activities for the week.

• If I read an email that makes me angry, I will wait 20 minutes before responding.

If-then plans assist in resisting temptation because they help you replace the habit you are trying to avoid with a healthier alternative (e.g. drinking coffee instead of eating a donut). Aside from helping you break bad habits, this approach will help you deal with distractions as well.

Creating a preemptive plan that is linked to a time, place, and specific action makes a huge difference in forming better habits. Evidence shows that this approach will make you two to three times more likely to achieve your goals! Here are a few simple *if-then* plan tips:

• Write your key action steps in your planner (or *Rise Journal*), including a date, time, and frequency—just like you would a coffee meeting or date with your loved one.
• Be as specific as possible about what you are going to do.
• Create a contingency plan for when common distractions or temptations pop-up.

This habit-hack will be a game changer for you as you stick create lasting rituals and strong, healthy patterns.

DEVELOP A PROCESS

While working with other sales professionals in my sales trainer role, I often ask them one simple question: "What is your sales goal for the month?" My next question is: "What are the key activities you must do daily, weekly, or monthly to make this happen?" I listen to their lists before offering my suggestions. My last and most important question is: "How can you quantify your actions?" Meaning, look at your key action items—how often are you going to do them, and when are you going to do them? This approach creates a "process," or what I call "daily disciplines." If you focus on your process and not solely on your outcomes, you'll be well on your way to achieving your goals.

My colleague, Scott in Kansas City, gave this approach a try and said it made all the difference in his sales results. When I went to work with him, we identified his key accounts and customers and how frequently he needed to call on them to create maximum impact. We selected several sales strategies and props he would use and how often he would utilize them per day and per week. Finally, we created a "story" that was specific to his territory and our product line. People buy feelings not facts, and storytelling is the best way to employ emotion in changing behavior. If Scott was able to secure a specific number of appointments, execute his core message enough times, and share his story, he would generate more sales. After two months of applying this approach, his sales numbers nearly doubled!

I know this sounds very basic, but the more simplified your approach, the less you need to worry about. Reduce the chance of decision fatigue and create a process. By adding a frequency or date to your action steps, you'll create more clarity, measurable account- ability, and results.

MAKE JOURNALING A WINNING HABIT

Scientific research suggests that it takes between 21 and 66 days to form a habit. Sorry folks, success is not a microwave but a Crockpot. It's slow-cooking. If you are seeking change and growth in your life that is consistent, you must make it a habit and practice that habit over a long period of time. So many people lack the patience to see things through. They are looking for instant grat- ification. Who can blame them? It seems everything today comes instantly: email, text-messaging, SnapChat, binging on Netflix, or buying things on Amazon Prime. Those vehicles of rapid response are nice, but we need to switch to a mindset that fosters endurance, fortitude, grit, and perseverance. We have to pay the price. We have to EARN IT.

Overnight success is not as powerful as success that comes from blood, sweat, and tears.

Knowing this, I have created a template that I'd like you to try for seven days. Once you've completed this book, and learned the impact that the GOALS V journaling system can have on your life, put this knowledge into practice. Take the *Rise Journal 7 Day Chal- lenge* and see how you feel. You owe it to yourself!

This simple five to ten minute daily habit can be the change agent that you've been missing. The *Rise Journal* has been my keystone habit and it's produced amazing results in my life. I want you to experience the same level of fulfillment. Give this system a week and begin to build a better version of you.

Once you complete the *Rise Journal 7 Day Challenge* in this book, visit www.theCollinHenderson.com to get the journaling book, *Rise Journal*. This version will give you all the space you need to update your monthly goals and map out your intentions to continue on your journey.

RISE REVIEW

Your discipline and habits are going to be the key factors determining whether you achieve or do not achieve your goals. Identify a keystone habit that will set off a chain reaction of good for other habits to follow. To take your actions and rituals to the next level, create a preemptive plan that is linked to a time, place, and specific action. Adding a frequency and a way to quantify your actions is another tip that generates better results. This strategy will make a huge difference in forming better habits.

Finally, by completing your *Rise Journal* daily for seven days (see the back of the book), you will start to embed a winning habit that will bear fruit, fulfillment, and a foundation for more good in your life. Continue that momentum with a *Rise Journal!*

CHAPTER 8
EXECUTING YOUR RISE JOURNAL

WRITE IT DOWN. WRITTEN GOALS HAVE A WAY OF TRANSFORMING
WISHES INTO WANTS; CANT'S INTO CANS; DREAMS INTO PLANS;
AND PLANS INTO REALITY. DON'T JUST THINK IT–INK IT!
-MICHAEL KORDA

There is increasing evidence to support the notion that journaling has a positive effect on not only our brains, but our physical health as well. The concept of slowing down, gathering your thoughts, and documenting them in one place is a form of mindfulness. This act of mono-tasking can help in many aspects of your life by:
* Clarifying your thoughts and feelings
* Reducing stress
* Knowing yourself better
* Tapping into your creativity
* Strengthening your self discipline
* Boosting your memory and comprehension
* Improving not only your IQ, but your EQ (emotional intelligence) as well

Aside from improving your likelihood of achieving goals, a report by the University of Victoria notes that "writing as a part of language learning has a positive correlation with intelligence." By utilizing your *Rise Journal* each day, you will not only improve the likelihood of achieving your goals, but this daily habit will help strengthen your brain. Signed me up for both of those!

I have seen a big impact on my life since prioritizing taking a few minutes a day to gather my thoughts, identify my intentions, and feel the therapeutic effects of journaling. In this chapter, I am going to introduce the effective use of your *Rise Journal* and explain why each individual element is important.

IT'S GO TIME

So now that you have everything you need to take off in your G5—GOALS, ACTIONS, REASONS, SCRIBING, and HABITS—the next step is to APPLY this approach daily. Under Armour founder and CEO, Kevin Plank, understands the power of application. Under Armour is a rare company. It challenges a market that has been dominated by Nike and Adidas for years. However, through Plank's leadership, Under Armour achieved at least 20% growth in 26 consecutive quarters (up until 2016). That is insane growth! What I learned from this transformational leader is that Plank asks his employees three things after every meeting in which new ideas are shared:

1. What did you hear?
2. What do you think?
3. What are you going to do?

Just like Plank's third question, this is where big things happen. It's now time to DO! So, let's get started. The foundation of *Project Rise* and your *Rise Journal* is the acronym GOALS V.

G – GRATITUDE
O – OBJECTIVE
A – AFFIRMATION
L – LEARNING
S – SERVICE

V – VISUALIZATION

Reflecting upon my life and my extensive study of what brings about success and happiness, I found that the essential elements can be organized into these five arenas: Feeling **GRATITUDE** in all things; having a clear **OBJECTIVE** each day; owning your self-talk with positivity through daily **AFFIRMATIONS**; investing in your personal development and **LEARNING** something new every day; and finally, being generous in **SERVICE** to others.

The true test of mastery is being able to take a complex task, concept, or idea and make it easy to understand. That's why I made this approach so simple. I've put in the work; I've done the research; and I've lived the process. This formula works, and the cool thing is anyone can do it!

One more daily discipline that will tie all of these five together is **VISUALIZATION**. Some might call it the X-Factor in turning your dreams into reality, but I like to call it the V-Factor. There are five letters in the word "goals." The Roman numeral for the number five is "V." The "V" stands for VISUALIZATION. This practice of mindfulness is a life-changing skill that will solidify the goals and actions to which you have committed yourself.

Having success in sales, I often get asked, "What are you doing to bring in the business?" Many assume I have some secret art of selling, handling objections, or a special closing skill. Honestly, using GOALS V has been my secret to success. Having clear goals and focusing on the steps of the GOALS V acronym is what has taken my production to heights never seen before in my territory and life. This is my best practice. I have used this approach to excel, and I want that for you as well.

This basic format will give you the guidance and template needed to get yourself out of a rut and into clarity. You will find proper perspective and fill your life with PASSION and PURPOSE. Commit to executing this activity and you will ingrain a habit that will aid you in tackling life's challenges and generating wealth in your finances, your experiences, and your relationships.

Each one of these areas is very powerful in its own right, kind of like the cartoon I used to watch as a kid—Voltron. When the

103

five individual lion robots joined together to form one unified robot, Voltron, the outcome was a force and a collective unit that could not be stopped.

All steps combined should not amount to more than five to ten minutes each day. Seriously, that's it! Just five to ten minutes. All athletes warm up their bodies before competition. Singers warm up their voices before they perform. Race car drivers warm up their engines before each race. You can't bake a pie or a pizza without preheating the oven. In order to get the focus and change you are looking for, you too need to warm up and PRIME your mindset before you begin each day.

You can work on your *Rise Journal* before you go to sleep at night, after you get up in the morning, or a combination (half in the morning and half before you go to bed). It really doesn't matter. What matters is that you do it.

For journal entry examples, check out the **Rise Journal 7 Day Challenge** section in the back of the book.

Take a moment and reflect right now. How much time do you spend on social media each day? Thirty minutes, an hour, two hours? Does this time really benefit you? Are you spending a lot of that time comparing what you have and what you don't have to others? Instead of waking up each morning and firing up your Facebook or Instagram, why don't you invest in you? Create intention for the day by capturing your thoughts on paper? If you spend just 5% of the time you would normally spend on social media utilizing a journaling system, you'd see that the benefits are transformational.

Find a routine and time that works best for you and stick to it. Before you RISE out of bed, commit to investing in yourself first. In order to serve anyone or anything else, you must get yourself right. The *Rise Journal* will give YOU the personal time needed to prime your mind, body, and spirit for the day.

The chapters to follow will describe, in great detail, the individual elements of the GOALS V journaling system found in the *Rise Journal.*

R

RISE REVIEW

The three most important words in the English language are: WRITE IT DOWN! Journaling and writing are tools that create discipline, intention, reflection, and clarity in your life. By having a system—the GOALS V acronym—to guide you as you prime your whole being, you will set in motion a force of awesomeness that will not be stopped.

HABIT #3:
BE GRATEFUL

IN ORDER TO BUILD A STURDY HOUSE
THAT CAN WEATHER ANY STORM, YOU
MUST HAVE A SOLID FOUNDATION.
BUILDING YOUR BEST SELF IS NO DIF-
FERENT—ONLY THIS FOUNDATION IS
BUILT ON GRATITUDE. WHEN YOU POS-
SESS A GRATEFUL HEART, YOU WILL
BUILD A MASTERPIECE OF A LIFE.
THIS CHAPTER IS ALL ABOUT HELPING
YOU TRADE EXPECTATION WITH APPRE-
CIATION. IF YOU CAN DO THAT,
YOU'LL BE THE WEALTHIEST PERSON
ON THE PLANET.

CHAPTER 9
G - GRATITUDE

GRATITUDE IS NOT ONLY THE GREATEST OF VIRTUES.
BUT THE PARENT OF ALL OTHERS.
-CICERO

It was January 2016. I had an amazing 2015 and just returned from our national sales meeting in San Diego. I just love these types of gatherings. I get to see many of my work colleagues and friends from around the country; we receive gifts and cool gadgets each day; we listen to interesting thought leaders and guest speakers; and our vision for the new year is created. It's basically one week-long party.

I received recognition on stage again that year as a top performer, which felt awesome, and I remember coming back home with a sense of clarity. I finally felt like I was in my lane and thriving at work. After going through many years of mental warfare as an athlete and sales professional, I knew it was time to share my story, but I just didn't know how I was going to do it. Thinking about this for several days, I finally had an epiphany. I was running on the treadmill at my gym listening to Justin Bieber's album *Purpose* (pretty serendipitous, wouldn't you say?). If you know Bieber's story, then you are familiar with how he rose to the highest of heights, hit a rough patch in his career and public image, then answered back with an amazing album and successful rebranding.

I could relate to this story arch. While reflecting on my previous year's success and feeling the after effects of our uplifting sales meeting, it finally hit me. I had already decided to start a blog but didn't have a direction for how I was going to launch it. However, listening to *Purpose* helped me find my purpose. On that treadmill I had an image in my mind and feeling in my soul so strong that I knew what I needed to do. This singular emotion was the one thing that was missing for most of my life, even though on the surface it looked like I had everything. That one thing I was missing was gratitude. Within a few weeks, I launched my blog *Project Rise* with a series I called **30 Days of Gratitude and Service**.

It took me well into my 30s to realized that happiness is a choice. One of the most powerful choices we can make is to choose to be grateful. With gratitude as my foundation for everything, I feel like there is nothing I cannot do. I hope to convince you of this mindset.

It's only fitting that as I started my blog on the topic of gratitude, that I continue to start each day by documenting in my journal an inventory of everything I have. Choose to be grateful—it's one of the most life-changing decisions you can make.

EVERYTHING STARTS WITH GRATITUDE

What if you woke up each day like you were a kid on Christmas morning? Or like it was your birthday? Or like it was Easter, and you were beside yourself with excitement for the egg hunt? What if we started each day with that kind of excitement and anticipation? What kind of energy would we attract in our lives with that enthusiastic and grateful spirit?

The problem is we get caught up on the rat race of life. We go to school or work in an environment we "kind of" like. We talk to people we "sort of" tolerate. And we continually compare ourselves to those around us and even celebrities whom we have never even met before. Then we aid and abet this constant comparing by equipping nearly every human in America above the age of 10 with a smartphone with multiple social media apps. Our self-worth begins to be measured by how many likes, comments, and followers we have. Somewhere along our journey, we have lost that wonder and excitement. We no longer anticipate something AWESOME coming.

Aside from playing the "Compare Game," many of us are living in "No Man's Land"—we have a pulse, but no passion. We wake up, eat breakfast, go to work or school, come home, eat dinner, watch TV, and go to bed. That uneventful cycle continues and repeats itself over and over again. Something happens in our brains as we leave childhood and enter adulthood; we censor ourselves. We revoke our own right to be really, really EXCITED about something, about anything. I certainly experienced this in my late teens and early adulthood.

I remember the summer before I went to Washington State University on a football scholarship, I had a conversation with my neighbor and speech teacher, Mrs. Chipps, about the new journey I was about to undertake. She said, "Collin! Aren't you so excited to be going to WSU? This is the BEST time of your life!"

I remember walking away thinking, "Everyone always says that, but I just don't feel it."

That same summer while at a baseball tournament I confessed to my mom, "Mom, I don't get excited anymore. I don't know what's wrong with me."

Looking back, I wish I could shake myself and say, "Open your eyes! You have so much to be grateful for! Stop comparing and worrying about other people's opinions!" I'd say, "Treat each day, person, and experience as a gift."

Fast forward to my late 20s and early 30s, knee-deep in corporate life, working eight to five in medical sales, and getting comfortable just clocking in and clocking out without truly recognizing what a blessing each day was, without making gratitude a daily focus each morning when I woke up.

Basically, what I'm trying to say is, many of us—myself included—have missed the beauty in the small things. Our lenses get shifted to focus on the bling, the accolades, the money, the wins and losses, and we miss sight on what really matters: people, relationships, experiences, contributing, helping, serving, appreciating

ALL THINGS and CIRCUMSTANCES. We spend more time in pointing out flaws and what we don't have, than discovering the beauty in all that is around us. We've lost the skill and habit of being GRATEFUL.

I remember before Kendra and I were married, we spent several months in a group pre-marriage counseling class. One of the main points the instructors emphasized was that LOVE IS A CHOICE. I believe that to be true. In marriage, we are tasked for eternity to internally decide to LOVE each other, no matter what happens. The same can be said about being grateful.

GRATITUDE IS A CHOICE. CHOOSE TO LIVE A LIFE FILLED WITH GRATITUDE!

Gratitude is the antidote to so many unattractive traits and debilitating feelings: jealousy, bitterness, hate, and most true for me, FEAR. It's virtually impossible to live in fear and be grateful at the same time. I challenge you to nurture gratitude when you go through turbulent seasons in your life. Often times, adversity and hardship are actually blessings that shape and mold us into something greater and stronger to better equip us to serve ourselves and help others.

Recently, I was struck by a post I saw on Instagram. It dealt with gratitude and read:

How to fail at everything in life:

1. Complain
2. Blame others
3. Not be grateful

The wisdom here is so good. To blame, complain, and shame is no way to live. Instead, have an attitude of gratitude. In the end, our attitude determines our altitude.

THE HAPPINESS ADVANTAGE

During my study on what brings about success, I came across

110

a book called the *Happiness Advantage: The Seven Principles of Positive Psychology That Fuel Success and Performance at Work*, by Shawn Achor. I even had the good fortune to listen to one of his lectures live on the power that a positive attitude and gratitude can have in the workforce. Achor, a Harvard graduate, researcher, and professor, stated that there are thousands of studies on anxiety, depression, and stress. Recognizing this, he posed the question, "Why don't we study people who are happy?"

The task was to research and document how people are happy and learn what characteristics these people possess. This information could be used to help others find happiness as well. Anchor shares that according to psychology studies, positive brains have a biological advantage over brains that are neutral or negative. People who think with a positive and grateful mindset perform better at work, miss fewer days, and are able to deal with adversity better than those who are negative thinkers.

Another phenomenon that Achor suggests is that most people think they need to achieve success before they can be happy. They need that promotion, that pay increase, a certain type of car, a significant other or spouse, status, a specific outcome or result, and the list is endless. Does that sound like someone you know? What Achor found was that this thought process is actually a fallacy and completely untrue! Look at the thousands of wealthy people who are actually depressed and hate their lives.

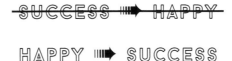

Achor discovered that when the order is switched, everything changes. When people are HAPPY FIRST, they will attract success much faster and sustain it much longer than the other model: achievement first, happiness second. So how does Achor suggest

111

being happy? BY BEING GRATEFUL!

Gratitude and true happiness come from within, not from external sources. Take ownership of your gratitude. Do not be like I used to be and fail to recognize the gift of each day. Take off your Compare Glasses and put a new set on—Care Glasses. Love yourself, be thankful for what you have, and be generous and serve others. This shift in mindset sets the stage to attract amazing achievement and fulfillment.

WHAT IS SUCCESS WITHOUT GRATITUDE?

After winning his first Super Bowl and MVP trophy, Dallas Cowboys quarterback Troy Aikman shared that once he got back to his hotel room after celebrating their victory, he balled his eyes out, asking himself, "Is this it?" He thought that after accomplishing the goals he had set for himself (success first), he would feel complete (happy second). "After winning it [the Super Bowl], all my problems professionally would be solved," he was quoted saying in the *New York Times*. His priority and his perspective were not in the right place.

This example teaches us that accomplishments do not foster gratitude and happiness. Fostering emotions of thankfulness and gratitude first will help you better appreciate and enjoy any outcome in a deeper and more meaningful way. You are not a better person because you win. You begin to be your best self when you understand the power of gratitude and appreciate any outcome as a gift to grow.

RELATIONSHIPS

What about your relationships? Are you spending more time identifying the flaws in your loved ones than the traits than pointing out traits that you like or enjoy? If this is you, you might also be wondering why your relationship is not flourishing, but struggling. Try this, focus on the GOOD in your loved one and be grateful for all of their amazing traits and see what happens next.

Now I understand if the person you are with is not treating

112

you the way they should, you have every right to handle that situation as you please. But if things are stale within your relationship, there is no spice or excitement, and neither of you is thriving, give gratitude a try and see what happens (also check out Chapter 13 on Service...then things will really take off!).

For all my single people out there, you become more attractive when you have self-confidence and humility. The reason you might be single is that you are focusing on all of the flaws of people who you attract. STOP THIS! I agree with setting high standards, but no one is perfect. Look for the good in others—inside and out—and remember, a grateful heart is a magnet for miracles in any setting, including your relationships.

GRATITUDE CHECKLIST

What if we treated each day with the awe and excitement of a child? The potential that each day brings and the beautiful little things we get to experience are what life is all about. Each day, each moment within a day is a present—the beauty of nature, the glowing warmth of the sun on your face, making a loved one laugh, feeling the rush of energy that exercising while listening to music creates. These moments should be as exciting and fulfilling as Christmas morning. We just need to make it an effort to recognize that beauty and joy. Most of us just don't take the effort to appreciate the simple things until they are taken away from us.

For the past several years, I have made it a daily habit before I RISE out of bed, to go through a gratitude checklist in my mind and write down at least one of these in my journal. Before my eyelids even open, I take a moment to think about the things I am so grateful for:
• My health
• My wife
• My children
• My family
• Our health and safety
• Our home

- My job
- My friends and coworkers
- Activities I get to do that day
- The people I get to help
- My Spotify app (I'm obsessed with music!)
- Iced mochas from Dutch Brothers (my favorite!)

Once this task is complete, I have created an emotional force that sets the stage for a productive and FUN day. Even when I am stressed or going through a challenging time, I try to focus on the good that harnessing that energy will bring. What other option do we have? There is not enough room in our brain for both worry and faith. You can only pick one. Quoting the Bible, 1 Thessalonians says, "Be grateful in all things." How does feeling bitter, angry, and blaming others help? How do those emotions serve you? They don't.

Try to see the good in all situations and look at the positives instead of the negatives. Take an inventory of gratitude each day and make it a daily habit. Then and only then, will you begin to RISE.

PROVEN BENEFITS

There are many articles and literary works that document the impact that living a life of gratitude creates for the human body. My favorite piece on this topic is an article in *Forbes Magazine* by Amy Morin, "7 Scientifically Proven Benefits of Gratitude That Will Motivate You To Give Thanks Year-Round," that lists:

1. Gratitude opens the doors for more friends
2. Gratitude improves physical health
3. Gratitude improves psychological health
4. Gratitude enhances empathy and reduces stress
5. Gratitude helps people sleep better
6. Gratitude improves self-esteem
7. Gratitude increases mental strength

There are many more reasons to practice gratitude than the list above. The obvious take away here is to find a way to make feeling thankful a daily practice. Capture each day (preferably in the morning) what you are excited about at that moment, and what you have to look forward to. This single act sets the stage for everything to follow. German philosopher Meister Eckhart once said, "If the only prayer you say is 'thank you,' that would be enough."

IT STARTS WITH YOU

Plato once said, "The first and greatest victory is victory over self." Loving yourself and being grateful for what you see in the mirror is going to help you get the body you want, the accolades you seek, and the loving relationships you desire. Practicing gratitude will result in a healthier bank account and the life you have always dreamed of. By focusing on what's around you, your current circumstances, and all the amazing things you are able to do, you will attract much more abundance and joy than you would living an ungrateful life. This will create a tidal wave of positive energy that over time will create the power to help you RISE.

RISE REVIEW

Get your day started off on the right foot by not only thinking about, but feeling what you are grateful for. This will be the single most powerful way to prime your spirit and set your day in motion to be the best version of you. Once you have gone through your gratitude checklist, write down what you are grateful for each day. It could be simple things like your family or health or something you are excited to do that day. Whatever it is, be intentional about feeling all the power that gratitude has to offer.

HABIT #4: IDENTIFY YOUR ONE OBJECTIVE FOR THE DAY

EVER HEARD OF THE KISS METHOD?... KEEP IT SIMPLE, STUPID? WINNING THE DAY HAS A SIMILAR APPROACH. IF YOU CAN IDENTIFY THE SINGLE MOST IMPORTANT TASK THAT WILL HELP YOU GET CLOSER TO ACHIEVING YOUR GOAL, YOU WILL WIN THE DAY. CHECKING OFF NECESSARY TASKS BUILDS CONFIDENCE. WINNING THE DAY BUILDS MOMENTUM. WITH CONFIDENCE AND MOMENTUM GROWING DAILY, YOU WILL BECOME UNSTOPPABLE. THIS INERTIA HAPPENS BY WRITING DOWN YOUR ONE OBJECTIVE EACH DAY, THEN GOING OUT AND DOING IT.

CHAPTER 10
O - OBJECTIVE

I'M NOT AN UNUSUALLY INTELLIGENT PERSON WITH EXTRAORDINARY
GIFTS. I'M A REGULAR DUDE WHO MADE A DAILY LIST OF
CRITICAL TASKS THAT NEEDED TO GET DONE. AND I DID THEM.
-ANDY FRISELLA

AIM SMALL, MISS SMALL.

I love this quote. This is a line from one of my favorite movies of all time, *The Patriot*, starring Mel Gibson. While protecting his family from British soldiers during the American Revolutionary War, Gibson's character, Benjamin Martin, reminds his young sons of this mantra before shooting British troops who have captured their older brother Gabriel (played by the late Heath Ledger).

This laser focus paid off. Through courage, concentration, and some serious sharp shooting, the Martin boys defeat the group of British troops, save their brother, and are reunited again.

That simple focus of "aim small, miss small," has always stuck with me.

Whether it's as an elite marksman, basketball player, or business professional, having a clearly defined target will serve you well, even if you're off a hair. I shared this story while providing sales training to a senior group of sales professionals. One veteran representative challenged this notion by saying, "Collin, it's not 'aim small, miss small,' its 'aim small and hit your target!'"

We both had a laugh and discussed the power of limiting your focus to one specific goal. This will serve you at a much higher level than trying to manage and process too many tasks and targets. This level of concentration requires incredible discipline and practice—but the payoff can be huge. The elite in any given field have the ability to focus on less, not more. This chapter explores this laser-like strategy.

KEEP IT SIMPLE

Many wonder why getting what you want in life has to be so complicated? It really doesn't have to be. Just look at it like this: *What is it that you want and what do you need to do to make it happen?* We need to focus more on DOING and less on WAITING. Stop thinking about the perfect strategy. You need to DECIDE that it's already yours and go get it. You might mess up. You might fail, but you'll learn a heck of a lot faster than by not taking action.

I've said it before, and I'll say it again: complexity is the enemy of execution. Now that you have your goal crystallized and written down, the next step is to get 1% better each day by taking small steps daily toward your goals. Think about it, if you got just 1% better each day—nothing more, nothing less—just 1%—add those daily wins up for the month, and you'll be 30% better than when you started! Add that up for the year, and you'll be 365% better! Just try to win each day.

So how do we win the day? By identifying one clear daily objective, writing it down, and doing it.

Notice I didn't say create a long list of things you need to accomplish, and do all of them at once. I said just have ONE clear daily objective…just ONE. You have already put extreme thought into what actions need to take place to make your goals happen (at least I hope you've completed that step in the previous chapters… if you haven't, go back to Chapter 4 and do this crucial step now.). The Objective portion of your *Rise Journal* is where you initiate the necessary actions to turn your dreams into reality. It's all about identifying what you need to do and then executing. Add this over time, and you can accomplish anything.

In early 2014, *Entrepreneur Magazine* published a story listing the 16 daily habits of the wealthiest people in the world. Below are numbers 12 and 13:

• They write down their goals
• They focus on accomplishing a specific goal

The wealthiest of the wealthy know; it's time you learn the about the power of having one specific goal each day.

ONE THING

No other book illustrates the power of identifying one objective for the day better than *The ONE Thing: The Surprisingly Simple Truth Behind Extraordinary Results* by Gary W. Keller and Jay Papasan. The One Thing has made more than 300 appearances on national bestseller lists, including number one on the *Wall Street Journal*, *New York Times*, and *USA Today* lists. It has won 12 book awards, been translated into 26 languages, and been chosen as one of the Top Five Business Books of 2013 by Hudson's Booksellers. What this long list of accolades tells me about this book is that it has a simple strategy that others have seen to be valuable and effective. Modeling your behaviors after other people's strategies for success can create a formula for your own success. Let's discuss the power of having one clear objective for the day.

Most people say they work eight hours a day, but are they really working those eight hours? With daily distractions like emails, text messages, Tweets, finding the perfect gif or meme, checking social media apps, taking multiple breaks, getting side-tracked by a co-worker or random phone call...you can see we have a lot working against our being truly productive. I didn't even throw in family and social obligations to that list.

To combat this, author Gary W. Keller, who is a mogul in the real estate industry, poses this question: *"What's the ONE Thing you can do such that by doing it, everything else will be easier or unnecessary?"* He stresses that the ability to dismiss distractions and concentrate on your ONE Thing, is what stands between you and your goals. By being laser-focused with your intention for the day, you will be able to get extraordinary results in any situation. When you are able to knock down that one domino, it will set off a chain reaction.

DOMINO EFFECT

Speaking of dominoes, did you know that November 13 is National Domino Day? Each year on this day, people all over the world create elaborate domino designs and watch with great pleasure as each domino hits the next in a rhythm and visual show that is both entertaining and satisfying. According to the book *ONE Thing*, researchers were curious to discover how much power and force one single domino has. Through their research, they figured out that one domino has enough force to knock down another domino up to 50% its weight (basically double its size). Then they asked, "What would happen if we kept compounding and doubling each domino in size? How big could it get?"

Once they got to 10 dominoes, it was the size of Peyton Manning. 18 dominoes, the height of the Leaning Tower of Pisa. 23, the Eiffel Tower. They kept going; when they got to 31 dominoes it was 3,000 feet above Mount Everest. When they reached 58, it was the distance between earth and the moon. That's one big domino! As you can see, one tiny domino has extreme and immense power—just like you!

This illustrates that by zeroing in on what you have to do, and doing what is number one on your list each day, instead of what's twentieth, twelfth, or eighth, you will create a habit of executing at the highest level. Identifying your ONE Thing and daily objective will set in motion the action and momentum needed to win each day and take you closer and closer to your goal. Just like anything though, this mentality takes extreme focus, discipline, and practice. Approach each day posing this question to yourself: *Is what I'm doing right now going to help me achieve my goal?*

Your one daily objective is part of your internal GPS (Goal Performance System). This GPS is similar to what is used when traveling, but this one is for your journey in life. If the actions and habits you consistently perform daily are not helping you reach your goal, then you probably shouldn't spend too much time with those tasks. We all get sidetracked every now and then, but those who write down their goals and focus on achieving them each day by honing in on their one clear objective, are much more likely to stay on the path to success.

CLOSE TO HOME

My wife Kendra is a prime example of how this approach is a game-changer for more productivity and satisfaction. After working for Amazon in Seattle for several years, Kendra had her sights set on running her own business, controlling her hours, and ending the hour-and-a-half commute to and from work each day. A talented graphic designer, she created an Etsy shop, called Hen & Co., to promote and sell her work (Etsy is a peer-to-peer e-commerce website focused on handmade or vintage items and supplies). She specializes in prints, invitations, customized cards, stationery, and apparel for moms and children.

Kendra even created a lifestyle blog to highlight her style, products, and our family. After moderate growth for a few years, Kendra was looking for strategies to take her exposure and sales to the next level. Like any small business, growth and profits take time. This was about the same time that I was consuming book after book about what brings success. I shared with her the power of positive thinking, having a clear vision through goal setting, and how creating consistent daily habits can take anyone's aspirations to levels not seen before. Two to three times a year, Kendra and I sit down for what we call our "business planning sessions." During these times, we discuss her goals and develop action plans that outline how she is going to get there.

Kendra writes down how many sales she wants to average per month, how many hits she wants on her blog, and what daily actions she needs to take. Applying this process gave her greater clarity and purpose, and she saw her sales take off. But it wasn't easy. Mothering four children five and under while running a household and a business is more than a full time job. I am truly amazed by

121

how she does it…I call her Wonder Woman!

To say things were hectic for Kendra after our third baby, Winnie, was born is an understatement. During this time, I shared with her how impactful creating a list and then numerically prioritizing her list can be. By identifying Her ONE objective and then doing it, I explained, would lead to simplicity, momentum, and most importantly—results. This approach would streamline her focus, I explained, and help her avoid getting slowed down by less important tasks.

Kendra was game and started creating a list then prioritizing it as part of her morning routine. By focusing on her ONE objective, over time, her business exploded. She now has achieved and even exceeded most of her goals. I am so proud of her! Identifying and consistently executing her ONE objective for the day has increased her sales, generated more followers on social media, and companies have been sending her free products to advertise on her blog. *Pregnancy and Newborn Magazine* featured our daughter Winnie's room in their January 2017 issue, and in 2016, Babble (a Disney company), ranked Hen & Co. as the eighth best Etsy shop for moms!

Kendra credits creating ONE key objective each day as one of the main reasons for her success. Put this strategy to work, just like my amazing wife, and see your goals and achievements explode.

TRIPLE "A"

Are you a member of *"Triple A?"* Do you have a *Triple "A" Card?* I'm not talking about the road side assistance one; I'm talking about the *Triple "A" Card of Action:* **Attitude, Activity, and Accountability.** This Triple "A" Card is similar to your bank account—you cannot take out a withdrawal unless you make a deposit and put money in the bank. Like my wife Kendra has found, executing your clear objective and taking focused action each day is like investing in your own bank account. It's similar to the power of compounding: the earlier you get started, and the more consistently you put in deposits, the greater and faster you'll achieve your goal. However, the longer you procrastinate, the more debt you'll create for yourself. Oh, and to qualify for this card, you must prove your passion, enthusiasm, and love for your dream!

STOP PROCRASTINATING, AND START DOING!

Let's break down what actions are needed to earn this *Triple "A" Card:*

• **ATTITUDE.** The first step is to wake up consistently with a positive **Attitude,** excited to attack the day with passion and focus. Do not let your environment create your attitude. Choose to have a winning attitude which will then shape your environment.

• **ACTIVITY.** The second step is all about **Activity.** See and be seen; hear and be heard. You can't achieve your dreams sleeping in and lying on the couch. Attack your daily objective with intentional, efficient, and effective action. Activity is the game!

• **ACCOUNTABILITY.** Any and all successful teams and individuals hold themselves **Accountable.** The only competition you have is you. Hold yourself accountable for your actions or lack of action. If you need support, tell someone (spouse, best friend, or co-worker) about your goal and ask them to HELP you be accountable. Make a bet with someone. Commit to pay money to a charity that you DO NOT LIKE if you don't stick to your action plan. There are even websites that you can log into that will help hold you accountable.

Here's another idea: find someone you care about to do the *Rise Journal 7 Day Challenge* with you. Psychologist Dr. Gail Matthews from Domiciican University found that of the 267 participants enrolled in her goal achievement study (I mentioned this research earlier in the book), 70 percent of the participants who sent weekly updates to a friend, reported successful goal achievement versus 35 perent of those who kept their goals to themselves, whithout writing them down. This shows that if you have an accountability buddy, the chances of achieving your goals double!

Identifying and executing your daily objectives are like the wheels on a car that will take you to your destination. Completing your *Rise Journal* each day will shape your attitude to have the right mindset and focus. Writing down your objective will help guide your activity, and also, hold yourself accountable. I credit a great deal of my focus and execution by writing down my ONE Thing each day. This step aligns my mind and holds my actions accountable to the most important person…myself.

ACT ON YOUR OBJECTIVE

Remember what the word **ACT** stands for? Action Changes Things. By executing your objectives and your ONE Thing each day, you'll create the change you need and the daily progress to achieve your dreams. The thought of building a house is a daunting task, but if you just focus on laying one brick, just one brick at a time, you'll eventually build something that provides you shelter, security, and significance.

All-time women's tennis champion, Serena Williams, uses a similar strategy. Before each competition, she writes on a notecard what her main objective was during her preparation, which will be her same objective for her match. This single focus helps lower her anxieties and limits distractions from things that do not matter—like the crowd, the weather, the chair umpire, and even her opponent. She also writes down a statement of affirmation to help give her the confidence to play at her best (I'll discuss the power of affirmation in the next chapter).

With four Olympic gold medals and 39 Grand Slam titles (23 in singles, 14 in women's doubles, and two in mixed doubles), I'd say that having a clear objective and affirming it has helped Williams. I have no doubt this strategy can help you too.

I can't tell you how impactful this one strategy has been for me. In being a husband and father, managing a multi-state territory, writing blog posts, speaking, and meeting people one-on-one while keeping up my fitness and friendships, I have found making my daily list and prioritizing that list has proven to be a weapon of mass production for me, and a weapon of mass destruction for my competition. This approach has also helped combat my fears, doubts, and laziness while eliminating the statement that drives me crazy, "I'm too busy." You are not too busy, you just don't have a ONE Thing! Start with the man in the mirror and make that change, like Michael Jackson sings. Have a clear purpose and objective each morning, and then watch yourself turn into a machine that gets better and better with each day. With your clear objective for the day, you will be one step closer to RISE.

RISE REVIEW

Review your Actions list that you already filled out. The Objective space is all about checking those tasks off of your list. Here's how you're going to do it: Each day, identify the ONE Thing that you must accomplish above all of else—and write it down. This will serve as your daily guide to keep yourself focused and on task. Once this objective is complete, move to what is next on your list, and watch the domino effect take off!

HABIT #5: GIVE YOURSELF DAILY AFFIRMATIONS

STICKS AND STONES MAY BREAK MY BONES, BUT WORDS WILL NEVER HURT ME. UNLESS THEY ARE WORDS THAT I SPEAK TO MYSELF. THOSE WORDS HAVE THE POWER TO KILL DREAMS. MASTERING POSITIVE SELF-TALK WILL GIVE YOU FUEL NEEDED TO ACHIEVE YOUR GOAL. YOUR BRAIN IS A MUSCLE, JUST LIKE YOUR BICEPS. IF YOU WANT BIGGER ARMS, DO MORE CURLS. IF YOU DESIRE THE CONFIDENCE NEEDED TO ACHIEVE BIG GOALS, PRACTICE DAILY AFFIRMATIONS.

CHAPTER 11
A - AFFIRMATION

YOU DON'T NEED PERMISSION FROM ANYONE TO BE GREAT.

-JUSTIN SU'A

You may have heard of this parable, but it is one of my favorites. When I heard it, it really struck a chord with me about how I used to live my life.

We have two wolves inside our mind going to battle and fighting each other every single day. One is a dark wolf. This wolf represents negativity, distrust, and fear. This wolf uses phrases like, "You can't do it." "You are not good enough." "It's too hard." "You are not worthy." "You should QUIT!" This destructive wolf exemplifies darkness and doubt. How do you drive out darkness? With light. However, light doesn't always win this fight.

In this clash of good versus evil, the light wolf represents confidence, gratitude, and belief. This positive wolf says things like, "You can do it!" "Go for it!" "I believe in you." "Whatever happens, you're going to be just fine." "You're a champion!" So which wolf wins this internal battle in our mind?

THE ONE THAT YOU FEED.

Jon Gordon, author of many books including *The Energy Bus: 10 Rules to Fuel Your Life, Work, and Team with Positive Energy,* says that the first rule for the ride of your life is to know that YOU are the DRIVER of your bus. Taking control of your life starts by taking control of your thoughts—most importantly—your in-

ner-voice. We all have an inner-voice that is working nonstop formulating opinions about our circumstance, environment, and how
we fit within it. Because we are human, we all have an internal
judge constantly comparing, measuring, and stacking up our abilities.

Our brain is consistently deciphering whether or not we have
what it takes, whether we belong, or whether we are worthy. Unfortunately for many people, including me for many years, we are
on the losing end of this tug of war of "I can" versus "I can't."
Sometimes our true selves aren't actually driving our bus. Often
our mind gets hijacked by an internal saboteur, or judge, that forces us to be out of alignment.

YOUR LIFE IS NOT GOING TO CHANGE UNTIL YOUR MIND, BODY, AND SPIRIT ARE IN ALIGNMENT.

Of the three forces just mentioned, which one comes first
and controls everything? You guessed it, your mind. It all comes
back to understanding that we have a critical choice to make. Do
you let the world dictate your mindset, or do you take charge of
your thoughts? Whichever approach you select will dictate your
world. Successful people know that when we take control of our
inner-game, everything changes. We do this by commanding our
mind to be positive, demanding our body to create energy, man-
dating our spirit to have courage and belief. Knowing this, we
MUST feed our mind with positive affirmations daily.

MESSAGE FROM MOM

Did your mom ever make your lunches growing up? Mine did. I
sometimes joke that I wasn't spoiled as a kid, I was loved. Not only
would my mom make me a sack lunch each day, but she'd also write
me a short inspirational and loving message inside my lunch bag.
Just a line or two of encouragement would make me smile and feel
better about myself. We can learn from this practice, but take it a
step further. When we are the ones speaking and writing positive

messages to ourselves, this activity will create an energy and out-look that will improve our ability to take action.

So what comes first?
• A positive mindset then positive actions?
Or is it...
• Positive actions, which create confidence and a positive mindset?

I can speak from experience that it most definitely starts by uplifting and encouraging yourself through healthy thoughts and self-talk. The biggest point here is that you need to just go for it and not let "perfect" get in the way of improvement and growth. By saying, "I can do this. It might not be perfect or pretty, but I am good enough, things will work out, and whatever happens, I'll learn from it," you manifest achievements that you once thought were impossible.

AFFIRMATION PROJECT

My earliest memory of giving myself positive affirmations amidst a trying and stressful time was toward the end of 12th grade. During my time at Puyallup High School, no senior could graduate without completing their senior project. This included volunteering a specific set of hours in the community, writing a paper, and giving a speech that was graded by teachers, peers, and a community member. As I mentioned in the beginning of the book, for most of my adolescence and young adult life, I was terrified of public speaking. I would rather clean toilets with my own tooth-brush than have to give a formal 10-minute speech.

After the embarrassment of stumbling, forgetting words, and stuttering my way through my sophomore speech class, I often worried whether or not I'd be able to graduate because of this se-nior project speech requirement (This was the dark wolf winning my internal battle.). When the time came for me to prepare my speech, I sought excellent help and advice from my sophomore speech teacher, Mrs. Chipps. Since I was a student-athlete, she gave me the idea to tell a story of my experiences through my gym bag. I would pull out multiple props and visual aids to take my audience on a journey of what I had done and accomplished during my senior year. That definitely helped, but one of the biggest factors that got me through my fear was that I wrote statements of positive affirmation on every one of my note cards. I put my positive inner-voice on paper. This little internal "hype man" was essential for my going big on my presentation and passing with flying colors. I wrote, "You can do it." "You're doing awesome." "Way to go." "Almost done!" With every new note card and every new declaration of written support, my confidence grew and grew to the point I was actually enjoying myself up there.

After this successful experience of using positive affirmations to my advantage, conventional wisdom would suggest that I would use this strategy to my benefit in the other areas of my life—in future public speaking opportunities, on the field as a athlete, and in my social life. WRONG! Because of my youth, limited experience with positive self-talk, and absence of a mental mentor, I reverted back to many of my bad habits sabotaging my brain with worry, anxiety, and worst-case scenarios.

Regret and guilt are obsessed with the past. Depression is trapped in a lifeless present. Anxiety is hung up on every bad thing that can happen in the future. Note: I am not a doctor and do not pretend to be one; medication and professional help are warranted for many people. With that said, taking ownership for our self-talk and increasing awareness of which wolf we are feeding—positive or negative—is a step in the right direction.

AFFIRMATION EXERCISE

When you hear the word affirmation, there's a good chance you might think of Saturday Night Live's character Stuart Smalley, who says, "I'm good enough, I'm smart enough, and doggone it, people like me." If you are too young for this reference, check him out on YouTube and expect to get a laugh. You might think this is a corny exercise designed for people who have low self-esteem—well, think again. All-time leader in Olympic medals, Michael Phelps, says he gives himself an affirmation every time he walks through a doorway. He notes that at the end of the day, he has given himself hundreds of affirmations, which helps drive him to be his best.

As I have learned, this technique takes discipline and practice, but give it a try and see what happens.

According to research on self-affirmation theory, Dr. Leslie Ralph, PhD, from *psychcentral.com* says, "When we engage in self-affirming activities, we are better able to handle life's difficulties and learn from our mistakes." A simple way to do that, Ralph says, is to identify your values and strengths. We will identify your strengths in a few chapters (Chapter 15: Love), but for now, take a moment to list your core values. What are your guiding principles that help you make decisions? What do you value the most that creates emotion in your life? Here are my values (I use the acronym BUILD because I am always trying to build and grow from my success and failures.):

MY VALUES

B — Believe
Belief is one of the most powerful forces—in self and others.
U—Unselfish
The best leaders and teams are unselfish.
I—Integrity
Operating from a place of integrity and sound values is everything.
L—Learn
I have committed to investing in my personal development as a lifelong learner.
D—Discipline
Hard work, winning habits, and discipline are the pillars of success.

List your CORE VALUES that will drive your behavior and actions. Try an acronym, if you'd like. Determining your core values may take time, but just like the WHY-Power drives your goals and actions, your VALUES underlie all that you do and become.

-
-
-
-

    Utilize this list to help you navigate your way through life and also to help you when you need to make tough decisions.

    When speaking to individuals or teams about the power of thought and positive self-talk, I often ask them to remember times when they were in the "zone" and accomplished great success. Take a moment to be kind to yourself and write down three things that you are proud of. These could be traits, talents, or accomplishments.

What are your favorite traits?

_____

What are your talents?

_____

What are your proudest accomplishments?

_____

Remember this list when you need a confidence boost. This list will also come in handy when you need to get your mind back on track when automatic negative thoughts creep in. As with those things you are thankful for, I encourage you to get these lists out of this book and onto your mirror where they can serve as daily reminders.

STEP BY STEP

I have mentioned before that the human brain is designed to survive, not thrive. It's made to avoid pain, fear, and danger. We need to know that the will to inspire our body, soul, and actions through uplifting thoughts can only develop by repeatedly making statements to ourselves like, "I can do this!" "I'm not afraid to fail." "I'm unique for a reason." "I've put in the work, and I am prepared." "I've got what it takes!" This is all true, but this is just part of the story. There is another key step here. You can give yourself positive affirmations all day long, but until you take action and start doing the necessary steps to do what it is you actually want to do (your goal), you're wasting your time. Here are the steps necessary to putting your affirmations into action:

Step 1: Tell yourself you can do it (revert back to the lists you just created above).
Step 2: Go do it.
Step 3: Grow and build from that experience.
Step 4: By completing steps 1-3, you will build confidence.
Step 5: When you grow and build confidence, you challenge yourself even more.
Step 6: When you keep stretching and challenging yourself, you will eventually master the task.
Step 7: When you master the task, you will feel extremely fulfilled and excited by your personal growth.
Step 8: Set another stretch goal and revert back to Step 1.

As you can see, a powerful domino effect is created by how you see yourself (similar to the domino effect I mentioned in the Chapter 10 on having a clear OBJECTIVE). I call this the **Delta Domino.** Another name for a triangle is Delta, which represents "change." That is why I picked the triangle, or "delta," symbol for the *Project Rise* logo. If you desire to RISE, you must make a change— mentally and physically.

THE DELTA △ DOMINO

▲ SELF IMAGE   ▲ EXPECTATIONS

▲ EXPECTATIONS   ▲ GOALS

▲ GOALS   ▲ ACTIONS

▲ ACTIONS   ▲ INFLUENCERS

▲ INFLUENCERS   ▲ HABITS

▲ HABITS   ▲ LIFE

With the **Delta Domino,** every change in a targeted area creates another powerful change in another area.

When you have a healthy thought life, or inner-voice, it sets off a chain reaction that creates life-changing momentum. What happens next is nothing short of amazing.

When you improve your self-talk, you then begin to upgrade how you see yourself. When you have a higher self-image, you raise your expectations. When you have higher expectations, your goals will get bigger and bigger. When this happens, you'll 10X your actions (as in increase your activity 10-times). When you change your activity and actions, you'll change who you surround yourself with (Remember: your alignment defines your assignment. We are a byproduct of the people we hang out with the most, so choose wisely!). When you are surrounding yourself with others who have the same drive and desire as you (or maybe even higher), your habits will naturally change. And this is where the not-so-secret sauce lies...when your habits change for the better, your life will also change for the better. It's a natural progression and cycle which all starts with your positive self-talk. It's time to reprogram your inner voice.

Your brain might fight this, but you have to keep saying these statements of affirmation over and over and over again until your body and spirit just follow and lead you to face new challenges with confidence. Many long-distance runners have a saying, "Don't listen to myself, talk to myself." Our natural instincts are going to tell our body to quit, give up, and avoid pain (the dark wolf). We must continue to ignore these thoughts while intentionally and consistently willing ourselves to feed the light wolf with positive affirmations. In order to make sure you are feeding the right wolf, you need to have a plan for how to do it. Your *Rise Journal* will help you make this key piece a habit.

Where I am in my life right now is a far cry from where I was several years ago. Even posting pictures on Instagram was an insecure experience for me. The things I have accomplished at work and in life—operating as a sales trainer, developing my *Project Rise* blog, and accepting speaking opportunities—are all manifestations of making a series of simple changes, which include my daily affirmations. If you would have told me five years ago that this was my life, I'd be shaking my head in disbelief. And here's the cool thing—I'm not done! I have so much more growing and achieving to do. I'm here to give you encouragement...if I can do it, you can do it.

AFFIRM, REPEAT

It's not what happens to you that matters; it's how you react to it that matters most. Ryan Holiday, author of *The Obstacle is the Way* offers, "The obstacle in the path becomes the path. Never forget, within every obstacle is an opportunity to improve your

135

condition." When adversity strikes, all we can do is brush it off, get back up, and re-affirm to ourselves that we can do it. This is not a one time exercise; it needs to be on repeat over and over again in order to conquer whatever challenges stand in our way.

Thomas Smith, author of *Successful Advertising,* suggests that it takes 20 times for a consumer to hear the message, pitch, or slogan before they buy. What is interesting is that Smith offered these wise insights in 1885! Advertising was still in its infancy, but marketing firms even today agree that more frequent equals more effective. Your brain is constantly marketing and advertising decisions to your body and soul. Be your own internal advertising executive. Be the boss.

CALL THE SHOTS. DON'T BE RULED BY AN IMPOSTER. OWN IT!

Commit to advertise positivity to yourself through consistent affirmations until belief is embedded into your subconscious.

This mindset is essential in all circumstances. When you screw up or fail, give yourself a quick pep talk to revert your thoughts and energy away from the past mistake, back into the positive present, and expectant of an awesome future. Whether you are an athlete, salesman, teacher, engineer, doctor, lawyer, garbage man, hair stylist, or nanny—we all are going to fail. Take a positive spin on the word fail and decide FAIL means "First Attempt In Learning." Keep lifting yourself up, not down. This is done by owning your inner thoughts.

Just the other day in a pickup basketball game, I missed three three-point shots in a row. The old me probably would have told myself to stop shooting to avoid further embarrassment. However, since I've been practicing using positive affirmations as a strength, I kept telling myself that I'm a good shooter. I even started to visualize the ball going through the net in my mind the next few times up and down the court. This tactic paid off. Down the stretch I sank four three-pointers in a row including the game-winner. Can somebody say, "NEXT!?" It's all about mindset and continual affirmations followed by action.

INCANTATIONS

Those of you who are disciples of the greatest life coach of all-time, Tony Robbins, have heard how he uses something more powerful than positive affirmations and self-talk. He uses what he calls "incantations" to get into the proper mental state to achieve greatness. Before starting out each day, or before one of his seminars in which he coaches thousands of people at a time, Robbins takes control of his physiology and mindset by repeating a statement of power and confidence while channeling energy from his body through movement.

Robbins learned this method the hard way. Years before he coached presidents, CEOs, world class athletes, and millions of people around the world, he had only a few dollars to his name. During this challenging time in his young career, Robbins needed to come up with a strategy fast to get his life on track. He often shares how this hardship brought him back to a pattern that he still uses each day to get his mind right. Fed up with being out of shape and out of money, Robbins got off the couch, went outside, put his headphones on, and listened to one of his favorite songs (*Heart's "Barracuda"*) while going on a brisk run. With each few steps, he told himself, "God's wealth is circulating in my life. His wealth flows to me in avalanches of abundance. All my needs, desires, and goals are met instantaneously by infinite intelligence, for I am one with God and God is everything."

While he ran, he repeated this incantation over and over again. Robbins channeled his inner power by developing a daily mental and physical ritual that focused on his desire. By using his mind and moving his body, he created a powerful mental and physical "state" to attack and conquer his goals. He said this changed everything for him. Why did this work? Because it gave him certainty. Whoever has the most certainty is going to win the argument or the sale. Improve your certainty by doing a similar exercise. This

137

strategy took his earnings from $38,000 the year previous to over $1 million the year following. Does this sound like a winning strategy that is worth implementing for yourself?

Robbins shares a line in his documentary called *I'm Not Your Guru* that my wife Kendra loves. He says, "I built this Mother%&#@er." Robbins built his brand, his wealth, and his success by telling himself what he was first, taking massive action next, and allowing God and the universe to do the rest.

Like T. Rob shares, the affirmation section of my *Rise Journal* is often my favorite section, because I allow myself to create a mentality and identity that I carry out throughout the day. I will sometimes pound my chest or even yell at the top of my lungs—usually when I am by myself and in my car. Your coworkers might think you are a complete nut if you do that at your desk on the job, but I'll still love you.

IT'S ALL ABOUT YOU

Find a time and place that is right for you to unleash the lion inside of you by making your affirmations physical with your voice, emotion, and movement. Jump up and down. Move your body. Go on a morning run or walk. Recommit to your fitness and while you are moving, channel the power of affirmations. Affirm to yourself with each movement that you are a champion and have what it takes. Find your own way to get into that winning state.

I highly recommend exercising in some form or fashion each day, even for 15 minutes. Moving your body consistently will prime your mind and give your body more energy as well. Whatever you decide to do, just find a ritual that works for you and stick to it. Your future self will thank you!

For my closing remarks on channeling the power of your inner-voice—remember what the author of *The Secret*, Rhonda Byrne, says about our thoughts: "We become what we think about. Energy flows where focus goes." Take control of your world. If you think you can or you can't you are right. Harness the power of thought. Use affirming statements daily to take action. Then watch the world bend and move like water to form the creation of your deepest desire.

RISE REVIEW

This is possibly my favorite section when I fill in my *Rise Journal*. Each day, write down a statement of affirmation that primes your mind and body to attack the day. Give yourself the confidence you need to combat new challenges by owning your inner-voice and inside world. A way to take your affirmations to the next level is to move your body while you do them. Learn from Tony Robbins the power of getting into what he calls a peak "state." Create a routine of physical motion and exercise partnered with positive self-talk.

CONSTANTLY ADVERTISE TO YOURSELF THAT YOU HAVE WHAT IT TAKES...AND WATCH THE WORLD FALL AT YOUR FEET.

HABIT #6:
MAKE LEARNING
A DAILY PRACTICE

ACCORDING TO BRUCE LEE, "LIFE ITSELF IS YOUR TEACHER, AND YOU ARE IN A STATE OF CONSTANT LEARNING." WHOEVER HAS THE CAPABILITY TO LEARN SOMETHING IN ALL SITUATIONS IS THE WISEST OF ALL. BRUCE LEE ALSO SHARED, "KNOWING IS NOT ENOUGH, WE MUST APPLY. WILLING IS NOT ENOUGH, WE MUST DO." WHOEVER CAN APPLY NEW LEARNINGS THE BEST IS THE MOST SUCCESSFUL OF ALL. IN THIS CHAPTER, I SHARE HOW POSSESSING A GROWTH MINDSET AND INVESTING IN YOUR PERSONAL DEVELOPMENT WILL FUEL FULFILLMENT AND ACHIEVEMENT.

CHAPTER 12
L - LEARN

TRUST ME, I NEVER LOSE. EITHER I WIN OR LEARN FROM IT.

-TUPAC SHAKUR

One of the fundamental shifts that has improved my mindset is the simple fact that I am never a finished product, but one who is constantly learning and growing everyday. This might be the most important piece of knowledge that I can offer anyone. I am so passionate about this topic that I made it the most robust chapter in the book. Trust me, if you can learn these concepts, you will improve your mindset and your life…I guarantee it. This chapter consists of two main parts:

- Part I: Retool How You Look at Failure
- Part II: Invest in You

PART 1: RETOOL HOW YOU LOOK AT FAILURE

Answer this question: do you love to win or hate to lose? During an interview several years ago, I was asked that very question. "Interesting query," I internalized, while I frantically tried to process this simple yet complex question. "Both," I responded to the bald-headed, dark-suited, rigid hiring manager sitting across from me.

"I LOVE TO WIN, AND I HATE TO LOSE."

The hiring manager, who resembled a bloated version of Scott Van Pelt, challenged my answer by saying, "You can't choose both, you have to pick one." "Well, I suppose I hate to lose then if I have to pick," I replied.

Let me preface that this was one of the worst interviews I have ever had. The hiring manager was one of the biggest jerks I've ever come across in an interview setting. He was hardcore, never smiled, challenged every single response I gave, and I let him rattle me. He asked me if I was a rule follower. I said, "Yes." He then quickly probed, "Well, do you ever speed?" I said, "Sometimes I go above the speed limit, I guess." He said, "So then you are a liar… you do break the rules." Cray-cray, right?

Back to the question of whether you love to win or hate to lose. The one valuable lesson from this horrific interview was that it exposed me to a really beautiful question that challenges one's core values, motivation, and fundamental belief system. As a sales trainer, I often use this question to explore a new hire's paradigm and approach to sales. Most often, these new hires and other people I ask, say "both." A close second is: "I hate to lose." Hating to lose is the dogma that has been ingrained in most high-achievers, go-getters, type A's, athletes, and sales people all over the world. Select sports, advanced placement programs, and special clubs are at an all-time high for children, and the ages for participation are getting younger and younger. As a select athlete at a young age, the idea that winning is the only option was implanted in my psyche early on. Many, like me, received self-worth and created an identity based on wins and losses.

To err is human, but to forgive is not the policy of this company. I learned from an early age that winning was expected and that losing wasn't an option.

During three of my first four years in medical sales, I received a phone call informing me whether I was able to keep my job or not due to downsizing and layoffs. Luckily, my sales performance was always good enough to stay employed. Winning and losing, in adulthood, becomes a matter of receiving a paycheck or not. This is true, but as I've become older and wiser, I feel like many of us are missing the point.

There is another group of parents and individuals who believe everyone deserves a medal, a golden star, and a trophy for simply participating. "We don't want to hurt anyone's feelings," they reason. I unequivocally do not fall into that category or agree with this set of beliefs. I believe this is a significant problem that manifests entitlement, complacency, and narcissism. In life, sometimes you win and sometimes you lose. You get the girl, or you don't. You land the job, or they offer it to someone else. You get accepted into the college of your dreams, or your application is denied.

The point I am trying to make is that failure is a key component of one's development. Two very different individuals, but visionaries in their own unique ways—Tupac Shakur and Nelson Mandela—are quoted saying a version of, "I never lose. I either win or I learn." So many people—including my former self—focus on the outcome instead of the process, or they focus on perfection instead of progress. If we spend more time channeling our energy in our preparation, attitude, focus, and effort, the outcome is irrelevant. Growth, knowledge, stretching oneself, and improvement should be the emphasis. If you look at goal attainment this way, trust me, the wins will come.

SEEK PROGRESS, NOT PERFECTION.

When you bust your ass, give it all you got, leave it all out there, and still come up short...there's nothing wrong with that. Obsessing over perfection will paralyze you. This approach of looking at outcomes from a different perspective might actually help you win more. Being clutch is doing what you normally can do when it matters most. Being able to lay your head down at night in peace whether you win or lose because you are judging yourself on a different set of criteria versus the W or L column is the only way to live. It's also the way to perform at your best. Judging myself on my preparation, being present in the moment, and leaving no ammo remaining—meaning I spilled my guts going as hard, as intense as I could with a purpose, passion, and a plan—is my only focus now.

If I lose, I can live with that. The next step is to evaluate where I fell short, adjust, improve, and try again.

Many of you have viewed losing the same way I did for most of my life—you give it all the power. This thought process forces people to miss the five-foot putt or choke when they have to perform in front of their manager or a really important client. When the fear of losing is absent, and you shift that energy away from the black and whiteness of a win or a loss and evaluate and reward yourself based on a different set of criteria, you will in turn be more clutch.

Stop giving fear the power! You are not defined by your failure but by how you react to it. Learn. Grow. Improve. Losing the battle is not detrimental if your focus is on winning the war—a macro versus a micro perspective. The power of perspective changes everything.

Life is short. Celebrate the wins, learn from the losses. Adversity, obstacles, and challenges often are our greatest gifts. I do not enjoy losing; I just look at it differently. My self-efficacy can be found in the E & G column (Effort and Growth), not in wins and losses alone.

So now my answer to the original question of whether I love to win or hate to lose is: **I LOVE TO WIN!**

Question: How you do look at failure? Do you see it as a defining event, or as an opportunity to learn and grow?

GET BETTER WITH GRIT

Every Wednesday night, I have the pleasure of coaching youth and high school football at a training facility called *Rise Football Academy*. One night at practice, I decided to show the high school kids a thing or two. We reached the end of practice and we were finishing the session up with some competition—a little one-on-one drill. It's pretty simple, the receivers try to get open by using the techniques and tricks that I taught them during their individual session, and the defensive backs are tasked to cover them and not

144

let them catch a pass.

Our defensive backs coach, Jeffrey Solomon (a.k.a. Solo), played for Washington State University just after me. He also balled out in the Arena Football League for several years. He is a beast, still under 30 years old, and could strap up and be an impact player at most DI programs right now. It's pretty awesome when your coach can dominate you. In the end, kids do what you do, not what you say. Well, Solo jumped into the one-on-one drills and was torching these young guys. Watching this, I got the itch to get in on the competition and dust off the old white boy receiver skills to show them how it's done.

In my mind, I envisioned myself like Julian Edleman, carving up NFL defenses. After all, I once was a four-year starter in the Pac-10 (now Pac-12). "I can take these high school kids," I thought, "I got dang near 20 years of experience on these guys. I got this!" I didn't have any cleats, no big deal. No receiver gloves, no problem. The fact that I had the norovirus the weekend before didn't even hold me back either (no food for several days...no biggie!).

My first rep didn't go so well. I guess I'm not as strong as I used to be. The second rep, I dropped the ball over the middle... where did my "sure hands" go? The third rep, the ball got tipped away at the last minute. I kept jumping in, expecting a different result, but instead of being Edleman, I was more like Pee-wee Herman. I caught only three balls out of 10. *Are you kidding me?! That's it...only three balls?...that's a 70% failure rate!*

When we finished, I walked to my car, pulled my hood over my head and zipped up my jacket feeling the cold winter-wind chill rush over me. I don't know what stung worse, the cold, or my lackluster performance. My legs were wobbly, and my ego was even less stable. This type of performance could have put me into official retirement, but this time around, much older and wiser, I approached this situation differently than when I was my younger immature self.

As I pulled into the driveway when I got home, I had already made the decision to give that drill another try. I envisioned what cleats and gloves I was going to wear, and even visualized a few routes that I knew would work. I walked into my house excited for the next time. I knew that my credibility as a coach and an athlete were not defined by that one failure. I didn't win that day, but I knew that the next time would be better and that I could learn and grow from that experience to attack the next competition with excitement and gratitude.

It's taken me more than 30 years to have that kind of a mindset. When I was a student-athlete or even in the professional world of medical sales, I had the opposite mindset. I felt like I constantly had to "prove" myself, which ended up hindering my performance. With each move or step, I would constantly evaluate myself and picture what others thought of me. I was constantly comparing. This mental approach no doubt hindered my ability to compete at peak performance. For many, past failures exacerbate fears of future failure. This cycle creates self-doubt and often anxiety.

These internal fears and anxiety lead people to give up, quit, or avoid being put into similar situations again. Thus, their true potential is never fully actualized.

Whether it is feeling super-stressed before a test, like a nervous wreck when your supervisor is evaluating you, or anxious before a big game or presentation, we need to acknowledge that nervousness, stress, and anxiety are all natural human emotions that we can learn to effectively address. Again, I am not a doctor and some individuals require medication to help with their anxiety and mental state. If you are concerned for yourself in this area, please discuss your mental condition with your doctor.

Research shows the brain can hold five to seven thoughts or ideas at one time. When the brain is in a state of anxiety, it can only hold two to three concepts. When we are operating in an anxious state and constantly trying to prove ourselves, we are operating in what I call a "Prove Mindset." Individuals with a "Prove Mindset" avoid failure, constantly compare, and seek validation in performance only. They have the idea that they have to "be good" at something or prove themselves in order to be a good person. This mindset is definitely part of the anxiety problem, and one that resonates with how I used to operate as an athlete and business professional.

Does this sound familiar to you or anybody you know, lead, or coach?

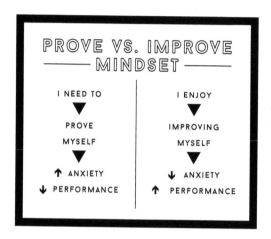

The goal is to have an "Improve Mindset." Columbia University's Dr. Grant Halvorson calls this a "Get Better" mindset. Stanford's Dr. Carol Dweck calls it a "Growth Mindset." Instead of focusing on PROVING yourself, try to focus on IMPROVING yourself. We all are works in progress and no one is perfect. Fear of failure is the enemy of creativity and performing at your best— no matter the area—professionally, socially, athletically, and so on. When your thought process is all about PROGRESS not PER-FECTION, what happens is powerful; you will start to perform better.

The best operate with the philosophy that they are not defined by their failure. What do you think quarterback Tom Brady was thinking after he threw an interception for a touchdown and was down 25 points in the third quarter of the Super Bowl? The reason why he is the GOAT (Greatest Of All Time) is that he learns from his mistakes, he uses them to grow, and he expects the best is yet to come. Other people's opinions don't matter, just his own and those in his locker room. Brady fails, thus he succeeds. He succeeds, because he fails.

Most of the New England Patriots' roster is full of rejects, misfits, and "failures" who are filled with GRIT. Someone needs to do a deep study on their model because seven Super Bowls and five rings tells me that Coach Bill Belichick and Brady have this Improve Mindset down to a science. This example should give you hope that if at first you don't succeed, keep grinding, keep pushing, keep competing, and your day will come.

YOU ARE NOT DEFINED BY YOUR FAILURE, BUT HOW YOU REACT AND GROW FROM IT.

University of Minnesota Gopher Football Coach, P.J. Fleck, has mentioned multiple times that he recruits kids who have failed. He looks for coaches who have failed. He focuses his entire program on surrounding himself, his staff, and his players with individuals who have failed and have GRIT—passion and perseverance. Talent does not beat skill. Talent might pass the eye test and win early, but skill is something that is developed over time. With an insane work ethic, and a thirst to win the war, not just the battle, you will improve your grit. Furthermore, this mindset will improve your likelihood of achieving your long-term goals.

University of Pennsylvania Professor Angela Duckworth studied and wrote a book called *Grit,* which is about the power of passion and perseverance. Many prominent leaders in business and sports are trying to tap into this new science of understanding GRIT, how to identify it, and how to coach it. Seattle Seahawks Head Coach Pete Carroll has even brought Duckworth in to speak to his team in an effort to change their lens on failure and persevering.

Grant, Duckworth, and Dweck agree: find individuals who

have grit, and you'll build a winning culture and team. This mindset retools how we look at failure. The statement, "I'm not good enough," should not be in your vocabulary. Instead, you should say, "I'm not there yet." This philosophy will help lower some of that anxiety. The threat of a loss will lose its crippling power. When you approach competition and life with a "Get Better" or "Growth Mindset," this approach turns failure into a stepping stone for improvement, instead of hindering your advancement.

So what happened the next week when we did one on one drills at football practice? With my newfound "Growth Mindset," I caught nine out of ten balls and couldn't be stopped! I used my previous failure as an opportunity to improve myself—not define myself. Walking back to my car after practice, my confidence and swag factor was at Level 10 because I came back and answered the challenge.

My hope is that you utilize this same approach. Never quit. Understand the term: fail forward. Failure is a gift—but only with the right perspective.

PART II: INVEST IN YOU

LEARN BY BOOKS

As I mentioned in the beginning of the book, when I moved to a new company a few years ago, I was assigned a mentor named Frankie. Frankie was very successful throughout his career, on stage winning national awards nearly every year. I wanted what he had and asked him how I could get there. Frankie was all about investing in his personal development. His answer was not to ask insightful questions, handle objections properly, or to "ABC" (Always Be Closing). Instead he gave me a list of about 30 books that were game-changers for him.

He said, "If you read these and apply them, the sky's the limit for you." After seeing the drastic impact just one book—*Positive Intelligence*—had on me, I began to feel extreme excitement as I considered the potential influence of the remaining list of books.

I attacked Frankie's book list like a white blood cell engulfs a foreign particle in the blood stream. I was all-in, and with each book consumed, I felt stronger and desired more information. *(See my list of game-changing books in the Suggested Reading section.)*

I made reading and listening to audio books a daily habit. The old me used to watch multiple movies weekly. I used to binge for hours on Netflix. I would spend extensive time mindlessly dinking around on my phone. When in my car, I would spend every minute listening to music or sports radio or talking on the phone to pass the time. Instead, with this newfound passion to learn, I made it a point each day to take in as much information as I could, mainly from audiobooks. I'm not saying the things that I listed above are bad, but I noticed that I was gaining more satisfaction (and still do) in growing my knowledge, skillsets, and the fruits of this daily practice.

This one habit of going all in on my personal development has changed everything for me. I couldn't have completed the content of this book otherwise. All of these accomplishments would not have been possible without making daily reading (or listening to audiobooks) a non-negotiable. I am all about non-fiction books... what about you?

Just think about it, if you have a 20-minute commute to and from work, that's 40 minutes of knowledge that could be gathered by an audiobook or informative podcast. During a five-day work week, that's over three-and-a-half hours. At that rate, you'd be able to consume about two books a month!

Everything we could possibly want or need has probably already been enjoyed by others, and most likely, someone has written about it. An endless supply of knowledge and wisdom can be found in the palm of your hand—a smartphone! Put Google and YouTube to use for good.

Smartphones often have automatic system upgrades, which update operating systems with the newest software. In order to get better, work smarter, and be more productive, we need systems upgrades too. This is only done by investing in our knowledge and applying what we've learned.

Did you know that the average CEO reads about five books per month, which is about 50-60 per year? Conversely, 25-30% of Americans read zero books in a year. The mean number of books the average American reads is five (this number is inflated by the small percentage who read much more). There is no arguing why the most influential and successful people in business and life read in one month what the average person reads in one year.

There are many proven benefits to reading:
• Improves mental stimulation
• Reduces stress
• Increases knowledge
• Expands vocabulary
• Improves memory
• Creates stronger analytical thinking skills
• Improves focus and concentration
• Improves writing skills

The top earners and influencers know the power of acquiring knowledge from books. Andrew Merle's article from the *Huffington Post,* "The Reading Habits of Ultra-Successful People" notes:

• Bill Gates reads about 50 books per year (one per week)
• Mark Cuban reads more than three hours every day
• Elon Musk is an avid reader and when asked how he learned to build rockets, he said, "I read books."
• Mark Zuckerberg resolved to read a book every two weeks throughout 2015

If these icons have enough time to make reading a priority in their daily lives, we definitely should, too.

Investor Warren Buffett calls reading the secret to his success. The Omaha Oracle says that he spends about 80 percent of his time each day reading. He tries to read up to 500 pages per day. Buffett says that reading is like compound interest—the earlier and more often you do it, the wealthier you will become!

I usually have one book I'm reading and one I'm listening to on audiobook at the same time. My goal is to consume and finish at least four books a month. While I read and listen to my books, I often take notes and write down the points that speak to me. Many of the quotes I list on my social media platforms are inspired by something I read or heard. These artists, authors, researchers, and creators definitely inspire me to innovate, face my fears, and be my best self. I want you to feel this crazy force of good and inspiration for yourself as well.

6 TIPS TO CONSUME MORE BOOKS:

1. Budget at least $40 per month on books ($10-$15 for written books, and about $15 for an audiobook. A monthly subscription to audible.com is $15 per month). Trust me, it will be the best investment you will ever make. If you are a manager, add this into your team's budget and let your team expense it.

If you don't have the budget, go to the library, ask your friends to borrow one of their favorites, or check out iTunes and Android apps, which offer free books. *BookBub* offers thousands of free or discounted books.

2. Use your phone, iPad, or other devices to **download books** to read (Kindle, Nook, etc). This method is usually cheaper than a hard copy and takes up less space.

3. Use iTunes or audible.com to **download audiobooks**. This method has changed everything for me. When I drive, this is my go-to to pass the time (or podcasts). Instead of mindlessly listening to music all day, get your mind right. I also use this method when I work out at the gym or go on a walk or run…remember, your brain is a muscle, too.

4. Pick a consistent time of day to read. While getting started, pencil this time into your calendar. Mornings or evenings are the most common times for me to read. I like to read at night when my wife is working in her office or when I jump in bed. This relaxes my mind and helps me sleep better (two pretty awesome benefits).

If you read 15 minutes a day, every day of the year, you'll read 12 200-page books in one year! A half-hour a day would bring your total up to 24 books a year.

5. Get some friends together and create a book club. You can do this at work or school and improve on personal development with members of your team. You can do a book study with a small group within your church. Or you can meet at Starbucks once a month with a few friends and discuss a shared book. I have done all three of these. When you go in on something together, it makes it more fun and holds you accountable. Be a leader and set in motion positive change by getting people together to learn something new.

6. Download the app Blinkist. This app has a digital library of thousands of books and reproduces them in summary form. You can listen or read the main points of an entire book in just 10 to 15 minutes! Most of the best-selling books and authors in the world are at your disposal. There is a small fee, but it's worth it. I get great new book suggestions based on my interests, which I love. With this app, I have read the essential messages of dozens of books that I have always wanted to read but hadn't had enough time to get to. Now with this tool, the book world is at my fingertips.

I definitely do not want to go back to that place where I was before I discovered the power of reading, listening, and watching new educational information consistently.

My hope is that you channel this same power and apply it to your life. Be curious. Feed that curiosity with knowledge. Apply that knowledge and reap the rewards. Who knows? If you read enough books, you might be a CEO one day.

READERS ARE LEADERS. LEADERS ARE LEARNERS. LEARNERS ARE EARNERS.

What is one topic that you'd like to learn more about?

LEARN BY MENTORSHIP

"Only two there are: a master and an apprentice." – Yoda George Lucas' second installment of the Star Wars universe, *The Empire Strikes Back*, brought us the most epic episode of the series, in my opinion. It also introduced us to one of the best mentors to dawn the silver screen—Master Yoda. In order for the main character in the story, Luke Skywalker, to conquer his fears, uncover his talents, learn the ways of the Force, and discover his true destiny, he needed a mentor. Lucky for him, he got one. A three-foot green dude with pointy ears named Yoda pushed, challenged, encouraged, and molded Luke into a true hero. *Do you have a Yoda in your life?*

Project Rise is all about being INTENTIONAL with our actions to move from a lower position to a higher one. Seeking to learn from individuals who are more experienced, seasoned, and accomplished than you is a vital part of your development.

You can gain wisdom in one of two ways: by experience or

154

by learning from others. Both are important. Which option seems more efficient? Learning things the hard way definitely creates great life-teaching moments. But for my time, money, and energy, learning from someone who has already been there, done that, sounds like a winning strategy to me.

I have made mentorship a competitive advantage at work and in life. When I changed companies and was four months into my new role at a national meeting, I asked around, "Who was the number one sales rep in our division last year?" Once I learned who that was (one of my favorite people of all-time, Roseanne from Boston), I introduced myself to her at the airport before flying home. While introducing myself, I kept it simple and said, "Hi Rosanne. My name is Collin. I am the new rep in Seattle. I've heard amazing things about you, and I'd love to learn from you. Would you be my mentor?"

It was not anything formal, but just a verbal understanding that I'd reach out to her a few times a month to learn what she does to be a high-achieving rep. Roseanne seemed excited and very open to begin a new mentor/mentee relationship. From that moment and to this day, Rosie has taught me so much—way more than I could have learned if I was riding solo.

Most people remember when they were new to a job and were just getting started. You would be surprised by how open people are to helping a new employee, or just people in general. I'm in my fourth year of my sales role with my current company, and onto my fifth self-assigned mentor (shout out to Frankie, Rosie, Jenni, Simon, Alison, and Rick). These relationships have been tremendously rewarding for both parties involved. My amazing mentors have pushed me to these accomplishments in a relatively short time: Winning Rookie of the Year honors, being promoted to a sales trainer, and winning multiple Top Performer awards. Having a mentor has been one of the best things I have done, and I encourage you to make this part of your process in becoming the best version of you.

I could not have achieved any of the success without my men-

155

tors. And here's another thing: you do not have to limit your mentors to just work. Life mentors are vital as well. So what's holding you back from having mentors? Here are two potential roadblocks:

You are too prideful to seek mentorship
- You think you have everything figured out, or
- You are too embarrassed to put yourself out there and ask someone to mentor you

Let me say that for those of you who bail on the idea of humbling yourselves and seeking peer mentorship, you need to get over it. You are never too old or too accomplished to learn from someone. Execs and leaders of all levels have mentors. We all can learn and get better, no matter our age, experience, or title.

You are worried you are bothering someone
- You feel like people won't have the time to help, or
- You will be a nuisance

You are not asking someone to do your taxes for you; you are simply asking someone to talk to you on the phone for maybe 10 minutes once or twice a month. My mentors live in Cleveland, Atlanta, Boston, Ohio, and Florida. We just connected via phone once or twice a month to get started and whenever we needed to catch up. I also have mentors that I meet face-to-face. Trust me, people have enough time. If someone says they are too busy, then they missed out on an amazing opportunity to learn from you. There's somebody better for you to gain wisdom from. Go into it with a positive attitude and expect this relationship to be beneficial to both sides.

Guess who mentored Mark Zuckerburg to Facebook dominance? None other than Apple icon, Steve Jobs. During the early days of Facebook, Zuck and Jobs would meet to discuss the best business and management practices for the young company. The advice seemed to work. Facebook is flourishing, and Zuckerberg's net worth is now over $5 billion.

Here's my challenge: Be like Zuck in seeking out a mentor early. Think of someone who has something you want, someone who you respect and admire. Think of someone you believe you can learn from. Ask them to be your mentor and see if you can check in with them over the phone and possibly meet occasionally for coffee or for lunch. And just see what happens. I believe you will reach your goals faster and on a grander scale by gaining wisdom and knowledge from someone who has already been there. Go for it! As Yoda might say, "A bright future you will have, if a mentor you choose."

Who are you going to ask to be your mentor?
When are you going to ask them?

RISE REVIEW

Begin to view failure from a different perspective. You are not defined by your failure, but how you respond to it. Remember what Tupac and Nelson Mandela said, "I never lose. I either win or I learn." This mindset will limit anxieties and provide the mindset that focuses on growth, not perfection.

Invest in yourself by committing to be a lifelong learner. Make a conscious effort to read, listen, or watch educational content as much as you can. We gain wisdom by one of two ways: by experience or by learning from others. Make learning a competitive advantage for you.

Another way to expedite your learning curve is to seek out mentors. Figure out what it is you want, and look for who already has it. Ask that person to be your mentor. (Note: you can also learn from mentors you have never met through books or informative podcasts or videos.)

You have two options while filling out your Rise Journal daily:
• **Option 1 (morning):** Before you begin the day, write down a topic, author, artist, or area that you'd like to learn more about and what method you plan on learning this information: book, article, podcast, YouTube, documentary, or mentor. You can use this section of your *Rise Journal* to reflect on what you learned the previous day (from a success, failure, or new information you intentionally studied) and how you can apply it.

• **Option 2 (evening):** In the evening (maybe before you go to bed), write down a key learning that you were able to take away from the day's activities. This key learning can be from a failure or a new piece of information you learned from a book or mentor. Remember to stretch your comfort zone and try new things. This is the only way you will learn. You are never a finished product but constantly improving and growing. Growth is where you will find ultimate happiness.

HABIT #7:
SERVE OTHERS

HOW MUCH WOULD YOU ENJOY SUCCESS IF YOU HAD NO ONE TO SHARE IT WITH? HOW FULFILLED WOULD YOU FEEL IF YOU LOOKED BACK ON YOUR LIFE AND ACQUIRED GREAT WEALTH BUT DID NOT CONTRIBUTE TO ANYONE OR ANYTHING OTHER THAN YOURSELF? TRUE SUCCESS AND WEALTH DOESN'T COME FROM MONEY ALONE BUT BY MAKING A SIGNIFICANT IMPACT ON SOMETHING BIGGER THAN YOU. ALSO, HIGH LEVELS OF SUCCESS AND WEALTH CAN ONLY BE SUSTAINED BY BRINGING VALUE AND SERVING OTHERS.
THIS CHAPTER EXPLORES THE POWER OF SERVICE.

CHAPTER 13
S - SERVICE

SERVANT LEADERSHIP IS THE ONLY LEADERSHIP
THAT ULTIMATELY WORKS.
-DAVE RAMSEY

What if I told you I had the secret to becoming happier and healthier with better relationships, more influence, and more wealth? This one strategy has been time-tested and supported by the most successful people in the world. This simple mindset and approach to life is this: SERVE others. Setting and achieving your goals isn't enough to satisfy you and keep you happy. Growing and, more importantly, contributing to others is where ultimate fulfillment is found.

Jesus washed the feet of others and died for our sins. Martin Luther King, Jr. marched for freedom. Mother Teresa fed the poor. Gandhi fasted for change. The greatest leaders of all time loved and served others. You want influence? Serve. You want more friends? Be generous. You desire more happiness? Help others. It's really that simple.

As I've been on this enlightening journey of discovery, I have found that we don't start truly living until we start giving.

I used to be a little on the stingy side. I rarely picked up the tab for others and didn't want to appear "soft" by my peers, so I kept my guard up. I rarely said "I love you" to my friends or even family members. Like many, I saw being generous and giving as a sign of weakness, or a pushover. This thinking couldn't be farther from the truth, and I am so thankful for the people in my life who have helped change my mindset. I am still a work in progress, but I believe I am on the right track. I'm doing my best to stay focused on serving others and spending less time being selfish and insecure.

SERVANT LEADERSHIP

Former Herman Miller CEO Max De Pree once said, "The first responsibility of a leader is to define reality. The last is to say thank you. In between the two, the leader must become a servant." Leading others and taking control of a life in which you make a positive impact and attract abundance is all about serving.

In the book *Lead Like Jesus: Lessons From the Greatest Leadership Model of All Time*, by Ken Blanchard and Phil Hodges, the authors point out that the word "leader" is mentioned six times in the Bible, where the word "servant" is mentioned more than 900 times. Many leaders and individuals who are self-serving, make decisions and act out of EGO, *Edging God Out*. There are many barriers we must overcome to be more effective servant leaders. According to Blanchard—who also wrote the bestseller, *One Minute Manager*—and Hodges, there are several ways the heart of a self-serving leader lets its EGO get in the way: pride, promoting self, fear, and protecting self.

Do any of these sound familiar to you? As I originally read through these, I know I checked off some of these traits, and I am working on getting better; especially in the "promoting self" category. Blanchard and Hodges add, "A heart motivated by self-interest looks at the world as a 'give a little, take a lot' proposition. People with hearts motivated by self-interest put their own agenda, safety, status, and gratification ahead of those affected by their thoughts and actions."

THE WORLD HAS ENOUGH SELF-SERVING INDIVIDUALS. WE NEED MORE SERVANT LEADERS.

One of my favorite servant leaders of all time was my head football coach at Washington State University, Coach Mike Price— who was gracious enough to write the foreword for this book.

Coach Price was the definition of a player's coach. I would put him in the same mold as championship leaders like Pete Carroll of the Seattle Seahawks or Steve Kerr of the Golden State Warriors. He truly loved his players, supported individuality, and always gave us a second chance.

I'll never forget the first and only time I fumbled the ball in my college career. It was against the University of Idaho, and I was back returning a punt. I was about to catch the football, but I lost the handle and it slid out from under my hands, resulting in a deep dogpile fight for the loose ball. Unfortunate for me and the Cougs, the Vandals recovered. I remember running back to the sidelines with my head down feeling discouraged that I let my coaches and teammates down. Guess who was the first to greet me on the sideline? Coach Price. Most coaches who serve themselves would have yelled and cursed me out. Not M.P. He gave me a big hug and told me, "Collin, you're our guy back there. Don't worry about it. I believe in you." That single act of servant leadership gave me the confidence to get back out there and make several key plays to help our team compete…oh, and I didn't fumble another ball the rest of my career after coach's life-changing response.

I will never forget the way Coach Price made me feel that day. The grace, the love, and the service that he displayed will stay with me forever. That's the way I want to live my life, with grace, with love, and with a servant heart.

Like Coach Price displayed, when you act from a position of love and sincere service, you not only help others, but you create leverage for yourself. Rank is given. Respect is earned. When your focus is people, positivity, and loving others for who they are and not for what they do, this creates a culture that is infectious and can turn average teams into great teams; low-performing schools into high-achieving schools; a life of scarcity into a life of abundance.

Make the decision to be this type of change agent in your family, organization, team, school, and community. Model the power of servant leadership, and you will not only be helping others, but

163

you will see tremendous fruit and prosperity for yourself as well.

SERVICE BECOMES PHYSICAL

There is evidence that serving is actually healthful and helpful to our physiology and psychology. According to Stephen G. Post, professor of preventative medicine at Stony Brook University in New York and author of *The Hidden Gifts of Helping*, a part of our brain sends out feel good chemicals like dopamine and possibly serotonin. These chemicals help us feel joy and delight, kind of like a "helper's high." A common reaction Post adds is that "some people feel more tranquil, peaceful, serene; others, warmer and more trusting."

At the end of each day, ask yourself this question: "How many people did I help?" If the answer is "many," that is awesome. If the answer is "one," but it was deep, that is amazing as well! Practicing generosity is one of the surest steps you can take toward a happy and healthy life. When you help a friend move, surprise your significant other with their favorite thing, help jump someone's car, donate to a charity, or serve food at a homeless shelter, the reward center in your brain goes to work and you feel good.

There are several benefits living a life of generosity creates that have been backed by research:
- Reduces stress
- Relieves pain
- Reduces mild depression
- Benefits your career
- Lengthens life
- Lowers blood pressure

Once you make living a life of generosity a habit, I promise you will not want to go back. There is no high quite like making a difference in someone's life. They say the best things in life are free, and being kind and nice to others is one of those free gifts... to others and ourselves.

My grandpa and most favorite person of all time, Don Henderson (God rest his soul), taught me that it doesn't cost a dime to be nice to someone. Grandpa Don lived a long life filled with happiness, positivity, and lots of giving. He was there at every one of my games, our go-to guy for rides to and from the airport, and he was "Mr. Fixer Upper" at our house. There was nothing he couldn't fix! In the end, he was the wealthiest and spiritually healthiest man I ever knew, which was evident by how many people loved him and how many people he touched because of his giving spirit. His legacy of love lives with me every day.

VALUE

In the end, it's all about value. Whether seeking a life partner, winning the sale, or having influence over others, whoever brings the most value wins. Entrepreneurs, business owners, teachers, leaders, and people from all walks of life who understand this basic principle are able to create wealth and happiness. The more you serve, the more you are successful. Develop a new product or service that fixes a need for many, and you'll create wealth.

The wealthiest men and women understand the power that giving and generosity creates. Whether it's Bill Gates, Warren Buffett, or T. Boone Pickens (all have donated billions of dollars to various charities, nonprofits, and organizations of their choice), the more you give, the more you shall receive. I was blown away when I learned that Andrew Carnegie, who was a pioneer in the steel industry and the wealthiest man in the world in the late 1800s and early 1900s, donated 90% if his wealth to charities and education. Carnegie understood how the universe works and was blessed because of it.

Matthew 6:21 says: "Your treasure is where your heart is also." Our generosity and "heart" can be displayed in several areas:
- Resources
- Time
- Words
- Actions

165

- Awareness
- Empathy
- Grace
- Forgiveness

Your joy, satisfaction, and in my opinion, one of the most important areas of your life—relationships—will transform when you serve. Your marriage or connection with your significant other; friendships; bonding with classmates or people at work; and relationships with your children, siblings, parents, and other family members will go to the next level when you serve them.

Do this exercise with me, extend your hand out with your pointer finger pointing outward like this:

I call this the *3x Rule of Service*. For every one genuine act of kindness, service, and generosity you give, you will be blessed three times over. The pointer finger represents one external act of kindness, while the three fingers pointing back at you represent the abundance of blessings you will receive three times greater than your one single act. Put the *3x Rule of Service* to the test. I promise, you won't be disappointed if you serve with a sincere heart.

GOALS AND GIVING

When you can clearly identify what it is that you want and who you are going to help along the way, magic happens. While studying one of the early teachers of attracting wealth, health, and happiness, Napoleon Hill (author of the bestselling classic *Think and Grow Rich*), I stumbled on a YouTube video of him giving life-changing advice on the topic of "goals and giving." In this video, filmed decades ago, he gave the audience a simple task. He said to pull out a sheet of paper and draw a line down the middle. On the left side of the page, write down all of your goals. On the right side, write down what you are going to give and who are you going to help in order to make your goals happen. This exercise is so simple, but so powerful.

After I heard this, I made my list. Now, it's your turn. In the space below, revisit and summarize your goals (you can never do this too many times). This exercise never gets old, but continuously reaffirms what your subconscious wants. Next, it's critical that you can describe WHO you are going to help. *Can you specify your audience? Is it everyone, your family, or a specific type of consumer or group?* Also, write down WHAT you are going to give that brings value to others. Take some time to complete this important step.

GOALS:

GIVE:
Who am I going to serve and help?:

What acts of service must I provide?:

SINCERE HEART

Former Director of Marketing for American Apparel and author of the *Wall Street Journal* bestseller *Ego is the Enemy*, Ryan Holiday, says it best: "Imagine if for every person you met, you thought of some way to help them, something you could do for them, and looked at it in a way that entirely benefited them and not you?"

If your heart isn't in the right place, you will not see the benefits of this way of life. The power of service only works when you really care about those you are helping. Also, you might be in a situation where you may feel your generosity is being taken advantage of. Feeling resentment or obligation will erase the benefits that we might otherwise receive emotionally and physically.

The Bible supports this approach of living a life of service with sincere intentions in 2 Corinthians 9:6-7: "The point is this: whoever sows sparingly will also reap sparingly, and whoever sows bountifully will also reap bountifully. Each one must give as he has decided on his heart, not reluctantly or under compulsion, for God blesses a cheerful giver."

In the end, God knows our heart. Serve, help, and be generous—but from a genuine place. Serving with the goal of receiving something in return is like receiving counterfeit money—it's worthless. When your heart is pure and your intentions come from a place of love and service, you and the world around you will be transformed for the better.

A WAY OF LIFE

While learning about the healing and rewarding gift giving provides, Kendra and I have tried to make lifestyle changes to make service a way of life. Once we committed to give consistently to our church, we saw changes in our soul and life for the better. God doesn't need our money, He just wants our heart. Just by making this simple change, we have seen abundance and blessing fall over us, including owning a home that we love, having four amazing healthy children, and living a life we only dreamed of. It wasn't the act of giving away money (but really is it our money? All that we receive is a gift.), it was that our spirit trusted and had faith that in God's economy: "He who is last shall be first; and he who is first shall be last; for many are called, but few are chosen" (Matthew

20:16).

While I am at work, I play a game of "how many people can I make smile and help today?" Opening doors, saying "please and thank you," giving a sincere compliment, asking people how their day is going, and being a positive light for others to follow is the only way I want to live.

When it comes time to pay the bill during a meal with friends, I love that I have surrounded myself with individuals who try to come up with creative ways to catch the waitress first to pay for everyone's meal. I don't always win, but I'm proud to say that I've won this game more than I've lost. When you surround yourself with giving people who love to serve with the same passion as you, you'll create relationships, experiences, and memories that will feel better than winning the lottery.

This giving approach has spilled into other parts of my life. I used to struggle with what to do when I saw homeless people requesting money on the street. In outside sales, I often spend most of my time in and out of my car driving to different accounts. I would often see people who have fallen upon tough times and are looking for help. There are differences in opinion about what to do in these situations, but I just made a decision to serve. If I am going to make a mistake, it is because I loved and gave…not because I withheld. So with the help of a few of our dear friends, Kendra and I have made care packages that include a bottled water, a granola bar, a fruit leather treat, and on occasion a $5 bill. Some months Kendra and I budget a specific amount of money to give to strangers in need. Often times that single act goes a long way, and in the end, the peace of mind that I didn't "swerve" when someone was in need, but instead I "served," makes me feel better.

SO WHAT CAN YOU DO?

How can you start this strategy of serving? Well, it's simple. Start at home. Serve your family, spouse, significant other, parents, and siblings. Serve from the inside out, not outside in. Model this behavior consistently and watch your marriage and family transform. When I do my *Rise Journal*, about 50% of my "Service" journal entries are ways I can serve my wife better. I am telling you, when things are right at home, it changes everything. Happy spouse, happy house. Treat your family like you are a peasant servant, and reap the rewards of royalty (Trust me, I'm not perfect at this, but I'm trying!).

Once you've got the hang of serving better at home, then move to your relationships outside your home—your friends, co-workers, and classmates. Invigorate your division, class, company, school, and team with energy and positivity by giving yourself and truly making the effort to help. Open doors, say "please" and "thank you," aid with little tasks like putting things away and picking things up, do the dishes, give unsolicited and sincere compliments, pick up the tab, pay for someone's Starbucks. Then move this mindset and way of life to strangers. Volunteer with an organization that moves you. Make someone's day by smiling and asking how they are doing. Treat the custodians and cooks like they are the presidents and CEOs.

The world has enough of what bestselling author Jon Gordon calls "energy vampires," who suck the energy out of the room with their selfishness and negativity. We don't need more Debbie Downers or Eeyores who bring the mood from a 10 to a 3. Serving creates energy. Energy creates positivity. Positivity creates prosperity. Prosperity creates change for the better.

LEGACY

I am obsessed with the concept of legacy and wanting to leave a mark during my time in this world. The game of life isn't about how many toys, cars, gadgets or how much money I can get; it's about how many people I can help, support, love, and inspire to be a better person. The question I ask myself is, "How many people can I serve?" Ebenezer Scrooge is a perfect example of this mindset shift. Once he was visited by the ghosts of Christmas past, present, and future, he realized that life isn't about how much we TAKE and ACQUIRE, but how much we GIVE and INSPIRE.

My motive is to leave a legacy of service and love that my wife, children, and others see and model. Love is the most powerful emotion one can give and receive. The act of giving yourself up and sacrificing your gain for someone else is the purest form of love. This single concept is why I do what I do—to help and serve as many people as I possibly can, while I am alive. This is also my hope for you. I hope that while writing in your *Rise Journal*, you see and feel the amazing difference of that giving yourself up, dropping your ego, and seeking to serve makes for others, and especially for you. My wish is that you make this mindset a daily habit. If you do, I promise, there is nothing that can stop you from achieving greatness and being the best version of you.

RISE REVIEW

We RISE by serving others. Servant leadership is truly the only effective form of leadership. Aside from creating more influence, serving has been proven to have immense health benefits as well. Each day, make a plan to help someone or do some form of service to help others. You have two options while completing this section in your *Rise Journal*:

Option 1: Identify and write down a person you plan on serving or a giving act you plan on doing that will help others.

Option 2: The other option is to know that this is one of your assignments for the day. In the evening, before you go to bed, write down what you did to serve others during the day and how it made you feel.

HABIT #8: VISUALIZE

PICTURING YOUR FUTURE GOAL IN YOUR MIND BEFORE IT HAPPENS IS LIKE MAKING A MOVIE TRAILER. THE BETTER THE TRAILER, THE MORE EXCITED YOU'LL BE AND THE MORE LIKELY YOU'LL GO SEE THE FILM. VISUALIZING YOUR LIFE AS YOUR BEST SELF IS LIKE MAKING A MENTAL MOVIE TRAILER: YOU CAN'T SEE THE FINAL PRODUCT, BUT YOU CAN SEE THE MAIN EFFECTS AND PLOT LINES OF WHAT'S TO COME… AND THAT IS WHERE THE FUN BEGINS. BY HAVING AN ENDGAME VISION, YOUR SUBCONSCIOUS WILL DO THE REST. THE KEY IS TO IDENTIFY WHAT KEY ACTION STEPS MUST TAKE PLACE TO MAKE YOUR VISION COME TO LIFE THEN VISUALIZE THOSE TOO. IT'S TIME YOU TAKE UP THIS WINNING HABIT AND LET YOUR SUBCONSCIOUS GO TO WORK FOR YOU. WHO KNOWS, YOU JUST MIGHT CREATE A BLOCKBUSTER.

CHAPTER 14
V - VISUALIZATION

IT IS ONE THING TO IDOLIZE HEROES. IT IS QUITE ANOTHER TO
VISUALIZE YOURSELF IN THEIR PLACE. WHEN I SAW GREAT PEOPLE,
I SAID TO MYSELF: I CAN BE THERE.
-ARNOLD SCHWARZENEGGER

You have undoubtedly heard of what is called the X-Factor. The X-Factor is anything that is the difference-maker in any situation, challenge, or quest that makes all the difference. Google's definition of the word "X-factor" is *a variable in a given situation that could have the most significant impact on the outcome.* This missing piece, when applied, is the key factor in making a goal actualized. Well, let me introduce you to the V-Factor. The "V" stands for VISUALIZATION. The V-Factor is the key variable that can have the most significance and impact on what it is you want. Visualizing your goals as if you have already achieved them is in essence the X-Factor in making your wants come to life.

I know this sounds all nice and full of self help vernacular, but there is real science behind visualization.

The brain thinks in pictures, not in words and sentences. When you VISUALIZE an action, this activates the same areas of the brain that awaken when you are actually doing that action. For example, when you mentally picture lifting your left hand, you stimulate the same part of the brain that is activated when you actually lift your left hand. For example, stroke victims who have lost function of an arm, can stimulate blood flow to that area, just by imagining they are moving their arm.

Whether we visualize it, or learn something new, our brain forms new neural connections that create sort of a mental map. The more we mentally rehearse these actions, the stronger the connections become.

For instance, Cleveland Clinic Foundation exercise psychologist, Guang Yue, studied and compared people who worked out at a gym with people who did virtual workouts mentally. He found a 30% muscle increase in the group who went to the gym, while the group of participants who did mental exercises of the weight training, increased muscle strength by almost half as much—13.5%. This average remained for three months following the mental training. This is fascinating—you can make your muscles stronger with your brain!

It's scientifically proven, the more you visualize an activity, the greater your chances are of making it happen. The more senses (smell, hear, feel, taste, see) you can incorporate while you visualize the better as well.

BEING MINDFUL PAYS

After interviewing over 200 successful people including billionaires, professional athletes, top-selling authors, and leaders in specific fields, Tim Ferriss, who has one of the most followed podcasts in the world (*The Tim Ferriss Show*) and is a *New York Times* bestselling author (including the *4 Hour Work Week* and the *4 Hour Body*), found while writing his book *Tools for Titans* that over 80 percent of the icons he interviewed practice some form of meditation, mindfulness, and visualization daily.

Belief and visualization are one of the life-changing habits that I learned while reading many books that share the power of meditation, prayer, and practicing some form of mindfulness. When you consistently allow yourself quiet time to be still, breathe, and be intentional with your thoughts and visualize your goals coming true, you will without a doubt attract more joy in your life. This is using the Law of Attraction to your benefit. It's worth repeating the concept that "thoughts become things." The human brain is like a magnet. Our very own circumstance is often a manifestation of our thoughts and what we see in our mind.

If you choose to think negatively, the results are catastrophic. Remember: "like" attracts "like." This means that negativity attracts negativity, while positivity attracts positivity. Can you think of someone you know who is constantly a victim and sour all the time? They always have a negative attitude and are constantly complaining that everything and everyone is out to get them. This very mindset is what is creating and attracting more bad things in their life. **You might need to gift this book to that person!**

Don't be like these people. They most likely have created a negative ritual each day, where they envision "worst case scenarios." Instead, create a positive morning ritual where you carve out quiet time to be in peace, meditate, or practice some form of visualization, which will prime your mind to attract more positivity and more good in your life. Who doesn't want more of that?

OMENS

What happens when you visualize the outcome as if you already have it and believe that the goals you have set for yourself will come true? This is where your brain's RAS (reticular activation system) comes into play. Ideas will start pouring in. You will notice people, strategies, techniques, information, and actions that will lead you to your target.

I love the book *The Alchemist*. Author Paulo Coelho tells a story about a shepherd boy named Santiago, who, after experiencing a recurring dream, decides to go after it. With a clear goal in mind and the outcome clear in his head, Santiago frequently receives what Coelho calls "omens." While following his "legend," these omens, or hunches or gut feelings, lead him on a journey of a lifetime and ultimately to his destiny and bliss—his goal (I'll save all the details...go read the book!). This story is a clear example of the power of seeing something you want before it happens. When you can see your goal clearly, your subconcious will help you go get it.

175

THE NOT-SO-SECRET SECRET

Another one of my all-time favorite books about being intentional with our thoughts is *The Secret*, by Rhonda Byrne. There are many books on this topic, but *The Secret* discusses in depth the Law of Attraction in a way that is so simple, yet so powerful. Not only is *The Secret* an international best seller, top selling movie, and shared by many successful people like Oprah and Steve Harvey, but this book is one of several literary works that discusses the power of the mind and our thoughts. I believe that God is in control of our lives and that He has the final say. However, since the days of Adam and Eve, God has given man the power of free will. Part of that free will is to choose how we use our brainpower and what we expect out of life. The Bible even says in Matthew 7:7: "Ask, and it shall be given to you; seek, and you shall find; knock, and it shall be opened for you." God is the editor, but you are the author of your life.

Identifying your goals, creating a plan, and having a clear "why" fulfills Step One. Step Two is to believe with all your heart and to anticipate by visualizing yourself living in the achievement of your goals. It's important to start with the end in mind and go "back to the future" with your thoughts daily. This act creates what is called a "neuropathway." Your body puts your thoughts into motion and manifests these energies and outcomes into your life. Energy flows where focus goes. Whether you cut out pictures or digitally make a dream board of the things you want (which I've done—I look at it every day as my screensaver on my phone) or simply think quietly to yourself, this strategy and technique is used by Olympic and professional athletes, successful musicians and actors, doctors, soldiers, businessmen, and ordinary people who are living the life of their dreams.

VISUALIZE, THEN GET THE PRIZE

Let me share a story that illustrates this phenomenon. While researching on YouTube examples of people who have used vi-

176

sualization as a success tool, I stumbled on a game-changing interview on the Oprah show. Broke and out of work, a young Jim Carrey used to drive to Mulholland Drive near the Hollywood Hills where he would park his car every night. During this time he would picture his name on the billboards, his face on movie posters scattered all around; he visualized his name on the Hollywood Walk of Fame. He said this act simply made him feel better and helped him get out of the tough times that he was experiencing. During this time when he hadn't quite made it, didn't have the money, or the success, he thought at the time, "They were out there, I just haven't received them yet."

He later took it a step further and wrote himself a check for $10 million for "acting services rendered." He dated it Thanksgiving Day five years into the future. He even kept that check in his wallet! Fast forward five years later on Thanksgiving Day, Carrey received word that he was going to make $10 million from his film *Dumb and Dumber* (one of my all-time favorites). Pretty awesome, right?

It is also important to note that Carrey added to this narrative by saying,

"YOU CANNOT ACHIEVE YOUR GOALS JUST BY VISUALIZING AND EATING A SANDWICH."

What he means is that it starts with believing and visualizing your goals as if you already have them, but you need to earn it through actions. Here's the cool thing, when you believe in your heart and spirit that your dream is already yours, even though it hasn't happened yet, this is where God and the universe supply you with more ideas and action steps than you can image. When these ideas and knowledge come to you, you MUST ACT! When you have what I call the Gift of **GAB**—**G**oal, **A**ction, **B**elief—you are tapping into a power that is like a freight train. When you go all in with your vision, faith, and activity, you will create experiences and happiness like you have never seen!

177

Like Carrey illustrated, you need to use visualization as a tool to achieve your goals. Once you specify what you want, believe and visualize that you already have it, then put in the work, the only thing left to do is RECEIVE it!

HOW I VISUALIZE

While speaking to audiences on this topic, I often get asked, "How do you meditate or visualize?" Many people understand the importance of meditating and visualizing, but they don't do it because they don't know how—they don't have a system. I share with them my technique, and now I'll share it with you. I have taken Transcendental Meditation classes and have been practicing different forms of meditation and visualization for several years now. I have created a template I use that allows me to relax and be more productive with my breath and thoughts. I'll share my three-step process that primes my mind, body, and soul to attack each day or challenge with focus and energy.

After I've completed my *Rise Journal* and processed what I just wrote down, I practice a system of mindfulness that I call the **3 G's to Thrive – Gratitude, God, & Goals.** I use this time to focus on three main areas in my life. This simple system helps me set the tone for the day and future. After I take a few minutes to quiet my mind, relax my body, and focus on my breath, here's how I execute the 3 G's to Thrive:

> **1. Gratitude** – I focus on what I am grateful for that day and "give thanks"on three levels ranging from small to big:
> a. Small (basic things like the weather, food, my favorite gear…just small trivial stuff)
> b. Medium (fun activities or events coming up)
> c. Large (my health, my family, my relationships, and so on.)
> **2. God** – I pray for people in three different areas:
> a. My family
> b. My friends and other people on my heart

178

c. Myself and for the things I want to accomplish

3. Goals – I visualize my goals as if I already have them:

a. Short term and simple goals and action steps (my daily objective and monthly goal)

b. Mid-level goals (my six- to 12-month goals)

c. Big, crazy, long term goals—I see all of these in my mind as if they are already done

DO WHATEVER WORKS BEST FOR YOU

You can use the approach listed above or you can use your visualization time to simply revisit the goals that you have listed earlier in this book or in your *Rise Journal:*

1. Your daily objective
2. Your monthly goal
3. Your six- to twelve-month goal
4. Your long term goal (three to 10 years)
5. **Your action steps necessary to accomplish your goal - MOST IMPORTANT**

Visualize these different areas, timeframes, and action items as stepping stones to achieving your ultimate dream. Simply imagine that you have already achieved those accomplishments and you will be well on your way to being the best version of you. I sometimes use the bottom part of my journal to rewrite my goals in present tense as if I've already achieved them. This practice gives me clarity and gets me excited for the day and my future.

Here's another tip to improve your mindfulness: check out the app *Headspace* if you are looking for more guided meditation/visualization options. The first 10 guided meditation sessions are free, so you can test it out to see if you'd like to continue using this method. YouTube and Spotify offer many free guided meditations as well.

GRATITUDE/VISUALIZATION WALK

I make it a point once or twice a month to go on a two-mile

walk near my house. This is no ordinary walk though. I call this my **Gratitude/Visualization Walk**. We live in a community called Lakeland Hills, which is about 20 minutes east of Tacoma and 30 minutes south of Seattle. This development sits on top of a big hill. From our house to the base of the hill is about one mile. When I go on my **Gratitude/Visualization Walk**, I listen to the same song on repeat: "Face to Face," by Hillsong Young & Free. The process of this walk has a great deal of symbolism for me. As I walk or run down the hill, I think about all of the things that I am grateful for—things in my life that bring me joy, as well as achievements I have already accomplished. Walking or running down a hill is easier than moving up it—similar to how I've already achieved the things that I give thanks for.

On the way back up the hill, I visualize and give thanks for things that I have yet to achieve—hence the symbolism of the action, hard work, and discipline that is required of achieving my goals in the future. Often I get so fired up because I have created a physical and mental "state," by moving my body while listening to music. The repetition of the same song is similar to having a mantra that one repeats over and over. This amazingly spiritual song keeps me in rhythm and triggers the emotions I'm intentionally trying to create: gratitude, happiness, joy, excitement, and vision. Sometimes I get so excited I literally start jumping up and down, clapping my hands, and even move myself to TOJ (tears of joy)! Once I finish the mile back up the hill of visualizing, I have primed my spirit to accomplish goals so big, most people would think I'm crazy.

This technique has done wonders for me. I hope that you can create a similar visualization strategy that moves you to TOJ from being so excited for what's to come in your life. Either way, find a system and routine that works for you. If done consistently, you will undoubtedly be more refreshed, have a clearer vision for what you need to do, and prime your mind, body, and soul to improve yourself and achieve greatness.

PUTTING IT ALL TOGETHER

The first time I ever applied the Law of Attraction and utilized goal setting plus visualization as a tool to achieve success was on Halloween of 2014. I'll never forget that day. I was six months in with a new medical sales company. Up to that point, I was devouring books on the power of the mind, our thoughts, and mastering our habits. I applied my newfound knowledge every day out in the field selling. The previous representative in my territory had brought in a high of nine orders for one month. Just in my second month, I generated 20 orders! My numbers kept improving, and by October, my production high had increased to the mid-30s.

I felt like it was time to really dominate and put the Law of Attraction to use. So, at the beginning of the month I wrote down that I wanted to generate 50 orders, which at the time had never been done before by a first-year employee. Most veteran reps across the country weren't even getting into the 50s. I didn't care. I knew the power thinking positive, taking action, and visualizing my goals daily could have in taking me anywhere I wanted to go.

So it came down to the last day of the month. I had generated 42 orders, just eight short of hitting my goal. The previous daily high I brought in was five, so eight would be a big challenge, but I believed I could do it.

I had made it a daily habit to wake up each day and first think about all of the amazing things in my life that I was grateful for— my beautiful wife, adorable kids, my health, my home, my career, and the unbelievable gift I had to help and serve clinicians and patients each day. The next step was to change my physiology by "feeling good." Knowing that my brain is like a magnet and like a cellphone tower, which needs to be turned to the right frequency in order to attract positive things, I utilized music to get my biochemistry going. Heading into the bathroom to get ready for work, I turned on my Beats Pill and started jamming to my favorite music. I can't remember the songs, but it was probably a blend of hip hop, R&B, mixed with a little Top 40. What can I say, I love music and love to dance. For me, there is nothing better to change my emotion than MOTION and MUSIC (Remember my reference of Tony Robbins doing incantations in my chapter on Affirmation?).

As I got ready, I remember visualizing what it was going to feel like to hit 50 orders for the month. I imagined what people were going to say, what I'd be wearing when I hit the number, and pictured myself smiling and feeling a deep sense of satisfaction and accomplishment. I had a huge grin on my face and gratitude was pouring out of me with anticipation of already achieving this lofty feat.

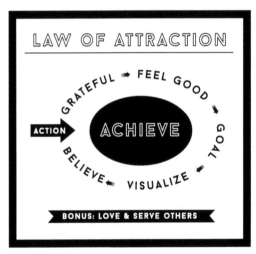

So I left my house on an overcast autumn day and attacked each account with great energy, positivity, and enthusiasm. Since it was Halloween, Kendra requested that I be home by around 4 o'clock to help with costumes and getting the kids ready to go trick or treating. The day zoomed by and it was 3:45 p.m., as I was pulling into our neighborhood. I was so pumped because I had seven orders and was one order shy of my goal! At that time, the last hour to receive order updates in our email was 4 p.m. I had 15 minutes left for an account to send in an order request to our home office, and my customer care representative to relay it to me via email (At the time, my go-to customer care rep was the amazing Tyler Bucknell).

As I pulled into the garage, I sat there in the front seat, closed my eyes, and visualized opening my email and seeing an unopened message from Tyler. Before walking into my house, I began to clap my hands with excitement, believing and knowing my goal was already achieved. I got out of my car, put my things away, kissed Kendra and the kids, changed my clothes, and honestly forgot about the number 50. Several minutes later, once I got settled, I sat down on the couch and remembered to open my email and check my inbox. Sure enough, there was a message from Tyler. I smiled, chuckled, and opened the message like a kid on Christmas morning, beaming with expectation. There it was, one of my accounts sent in an order, and I HAD DONE IT! FIFTY ORDERS IN ONE MONTH!

Saying I was pumped was an understatement. I'll never forget that feeling. That single event changed everything for me. I felt like I just discovered something so powerful but not taught in school or in business training—and anyone can do it! I want you to experience that feeling for yourself. You have so much control, authority, and command in your life. There is a lion inside of you, a giant that is just waiting to be awakened. Harness the power of setting clear goals. Utilize the proven effects of taking massive action. Let the laws of the universe and God's love come to life by visualizing your goals as if you already have them. You simply need to identify what it is you want, believe, trust your omens, and take action. Apply these concepts daily, and you too will generate feelings of exuberance and exhilaration just like I did the day I hit 50 orders.

NOTE THAT YOU CANNOT SPELL "ATTRACTION" WITHOUT ACTION…VISUALIZING THEN TAKING ACTION IS A MUST!

I've utilized this strategy to create fulfillment and a sense of accomplishment that I've never felt before. Now I crave it! From a career perspective, I have been handsomely rewarded by implementing this approach:

- Set clear daily, monthly, and yearly goals
- Create an action plan and then execute it
- Wake up with a sense of gratitude each day
- Visualize my goals as if I already have them
- Believe with all my heart that I will achieve my goals
- Do my best to love and serve others daily

This is my proven blueprint that I want you to apply as well. With my current company, I have earned the Rookie of the Year award, been promoted to a sales trainer (on top of my duties as a sales representative), earned multiple Top Performer awards, and have set new sales records never seen before in my territory and company—one of which I am very proud of, the highest number of product orders in one year. Before achieving any of these feats, I first set them as goals and consistently visualized them as if I had already achieved them, including what I was wearing, how it would feel, who was around me when I won, and what positive statements people would be saying about me.

As I mentioned earlier, the most product orders the previous representative in my territory generated in one month was nine. If you averaged that out for one year it would be a total of 108. In my second full year, I generated over 1,000 orders! That is a 1,000 percent increase! I want you to see this same kind of explosion of achievement and happiness in your life. Whether it's your relationships, health, or career (like the example I just shared), this system just flat-out works. Commit to this process, implement it, and trust it. You will be rewarded if you do.

RISE REVIEW

Once you have filled out the GOALS sections of your *Rise Journal*, take time to focus on your breathing and visualize all your goals coming true. Carving out this time will be your secret weapon that turns your goals into reality.

Another thing I like to do is to rewrite my goals in present tense (in shorter form). You will create a pathway to success just by rewriting your goals and taking time to meditate on those accomplishments as if you have already achieved them.

CHAPTER 15
LOVE

DO MORE OF WHAT MAKES YOU AWESOME.

I heard an alarming fact the other day. Guess what day of the week is reported to have the most heart attacks...more than any other day? Think about it. The answer is Monday. When this data was analyzed even closer, the time of day is also disturbing: 9 a.m. Monday morning at 9 a.m. is the most frequently reported time for heart attacks. So why is this? The only logical conclusion is that people are living with anxiety and stress about how they see themselves, their lives, and what they do in their careers Monday through Friday. Many people are not living with self-love or pursuing a life and career that they truly enjoy. This section of the book is all about being very intentional of discovering your strengths and doing more of what you love to do.

I am going to break this chapter down into three parts which all focus on tapping into your passion:
- **Part I** is all about how to LOVE How You Are Made
- **Part II** looks into identifying What You LOVE to Do
- **Part III** focuses on being more intentional to LOVE the Little Things

PART I: LOVE HOW YOU ARE MADE

Since I have a multi-state territory, I often have the pleasure of seeing friends and family along my many sales trips. Montana is one of my favorite places to visit because of its beauty, landscape, and many amazing people—including my dear friends from college, Matt and Sara Kegel. Matt and I played football together at WSU and were roommates our freshman year. The Kegels have a cabin on one of the most picturesque sites in the world, Holter Lake, which is about an hour south of Great Falls.

One visit this past summer reminded me of an internal voice that used to plague me. After swimming with the kids and going on an amazing boat ride filled with wildlife—mountain goats, bald eagles, a mother deer and fawn—rolling hills, and mountains so beautiful you'd swear you'd died and gone to heaven (They say Montana is God's country.), I found myself falling back into an old habit. Once we got back inside the cabin, I caught a glimpse of myself in the mirror. My vanity and insecurities popped up again. I looked in the mirror and thought, "Dang, my hair sure looks on the thin side right now…I wish I had hair like Matt." I guess that's what swimming in the lake and going 45 mph on a boat will do to you (a place you wouldn't find Donald Trump without a hat).

Most people, and DEFINITELY most guys, are too prideful to discuss or bring up things about themselves that they are not happy with. As flawed humans we are consumed and often times obsessed with our blemishes instead of focusing on and playing up our strengths. For many years, I was one of those people. I could have dozens of outstanding qualities, but like many people, I'd base a majority of my self-worth and self-efficacy (or lack thereof) on what I thought other people perceived as flaws. If you can relate to this, do a *Zoolander* "Blue Steel" look for me— *"Hansel, so hot right now!"*

Many, like I do sometimes, fall into the trap of comparing one isolated area that we feel is inferior to somebody else—whether it's related to appearance, skillset, character trait, or circumstance. Many take it to a very unhealthy place and use what they see on TV, movies, magazines, and now more than ever, social media as their barometer for how they should look, act, and feel.

I'm here to encourage you to stop those thoughts. Instead, focus on the strengths, character traits, and physical features that are unique to you and special compared to others. God made you just the way you are supposed to be. If you are living your life constantly comparing, snap out of it! I do not care how attractive or how good someone looks; even Brad Pitt and Gigi Hadid look in the mirror and don't like something about themselves.

True beauty is in the eyes of the beholder, and the most important beholder is you. Insecurities and self-defeating thoughts will only hold you back from being the best version of you. Focusing on your flaws is an endless game that you cannot win. Guess what…we all are flawed. We all have things about ourselves that we don't like—no matter who we are. Here's the thing, if you fall into this camp and are really unhappy with something about yourself then DO SOMETHING ABOUT IT. STOP COMPLAINING AND FEELING DEFEATED!

Confidence is not "they will like me." Confidence is "I'll be fine if they don't." Rather than focusing on our physical appearance, we need to spend more time focusing on what we are good at, our natural abilities and specialized skills or traits. If we continue to compare ourselves to everyone else and think we need to be an expert in everything, that's another recipe for disaster.

Strengths are the great equalizer. When you meet someone for the first time, have an important business meeting with a new client, or come across somebody that possesses a skill that you do not, just remember that you too have a unique set of skills that they do not have. They are no better or worse than you—just different. This shift in how you perceive yourself and others is life-changing.

A *Harvard Business Review* study revealed interesting research on how humans perceive themselves versus others. A research group created a study in which they introduced people to someone new and asked them how they perceived the other person. Person #1 usually responded by giving feedback that they felt lesser or inferior to person #2.

An interesting finding was that when they asked person #2 the same question, they gave similar feedback about person #1—

they perceived that person as more affluent, more put-together, or smarter than them. Wow, right? Now I know why girls always say, "She looked at me funny." That's probably because the girl was actually thinking, "Hmm, she is really cute."

Having three daughters, I love this quote from Mohadesa Najumi, which I found on Pinterest,

"THE WOMAN WHO DOES NOT REQUIRE VALIDATION FROM ANYONE IS THE MOST FEARED INDIVIDUAL ON THE PLANET."

Start taking control of how you see yourself. If you fall into the pattern of focusing on your flaws, make today the day you spend time highlighting your strengths and being grateful for how you are unique. And remember: you can't change the world if you are like everybody else!

Love Yourself Challenge: Write down one physical trait that you like the most about yourself:

PART II - IDENTIFYING WHAT YOU LOVE TO DO

Think about a moment in your life when you were in the "zone." Reflect on a time when you were filled with energy, when the right decisions came easily, when you were truly PRESENT in the moment. During this time, you were creative without trying. You felt completely fulfilled.

These moments, unfortunately, don't come as often as we would like. What if your job or role was doing that activity all the time? This is called playing to your strengths.

Many people fail because they lack self-awareness—they are focusing on the wrong things and not going all in on what they are good at and deeply enjoy.

190

Playing to your strengths sounds simple, but most people do not live in this zone. Gallup Press, a leader in strength development, found that less than 20% of people play to their strengths. Why is this? Well, life happens. We go to school and most of the time our parents and teachers spend a majority of the time focusing on our weaknesses.

A group of parents were asked this question: Your child comes home with a report card, which shows several subjects where they earned high grades and one subject where they receive a low grade—how would you handle it? Seventy-seven percent of the parents said they would spend all of their time and energy on the subject where their child is low.

Now I'm not saying that settling for bad grades is OK; it's definitely not. But in life, investing time, money, and energy on something you are not good at or you don't enjoy might not be the best use of your valuable resources. Many believe that they can gain the most growth in their areas of weakness. That is not totally true. Actually, it has been studied that people develop the most in their areas of strength.

Entrepreneur extraordinaire Gary Vaynerchuk offers this wisdom, "I suck at 99 percent of stuff, but I go all out on that one percent I am good at."

The more I study game-changing people, like Gary V., the more I'm led to this simple mindset and strategy: play to your strengths, and don't get overly consumed by your weaknesses. The most successful leaders, teachers, coaches, and managers understand this principle. They are able to get the most out of their constituents because they look for the strengths in their people and play to them. This approach helps people feel inspired, engaged, and more valuable...thus, it increases success.

Think about what you are really good at and love doing at your job or in school. We all have things we don't enjoy. But we also have activities that fill us up. What if we got so good at the parts we enjoy that we create leverage for ourselves? We become such experts and assets in our strengths that our companies, teams, or organizations—or even a new company or organization—asks you to do more of it…maybe even make that one thing (what you love to do) something you do everyday!

IT'S A MYTH

There are two myths people believe about themselves, according to Marcus Buckingham, author, speaker, and expert in the field of developing one's strengths:

1. As you grow older, you change.
2. You grow the most in the areas you are the weakest.

We definitely improve and evolve, but at the core of who we are—what we enjoy, our disposition, what we gravitate to, what stimulates us, what gives us energy and satisfaction and taps into our imagination—doesn't change a great deal from when we were children.

Vanessa Van Edwards, who is the lead researcher at The Science of People, and author of the book *Captivate: The Science of Succeeding with People*, notes that between 35-55% of our personality is predetermined through our hardwiring and DNA. What I'm trying to figure out is why a large number of people in our society obsess over their weaknesses instead of finding ways to enhance their strengths?

For many, their survival instinct is stronger than their success instinct. We often fall into the survival trap of life for several reasons: we graduate and get to get a job; we have bills to pay; we are pressured to live a certain lifestyle by family, close friends, or a significant other or spouse. And then the cycle continues. It's time to stop that cycle now.

Albert Einstein once said, "Everyone is a genius. But if you judge a fish on its ability to climb a tree, it will live its whole life believing that it is stupid." Don't seek to simply survive. Seek to succeed!

So how can you have success that lasts? Build on your strengths. Leverage your strengths. Commit to your strengths!

You might be thinking, "All right, Collin. I hear you, focus on my strengths. I get it. But, I'm not totally clear about what my strengths are." If this is you, think of strengths as not only what you are good at, but also:
- What you deeply enjoy doing
- What comes easily to you
- What makes you feel fulfilled
- What you never get tired of
- What activity you wish was your sole career

When speaking to a large audience, Steve Jobs said you must be passionate about what you are doing if you want to have success. If you are not, you will fail because the grind is real; there are setbacks, challenges, and adversities. Doing what we love, believe in, and are passionate about will help us stay on that straight path of growth, fulfillment, and achievement. Whether it's music, investing, makeup, baking, sales, cutting grass, problem-solving, fixing, teaching, building, connecting people, serving others—do more of what makes you awesome, because if you do: YOU CAN MAKE A LIVING AND A LIFE DOING WHAT YOU LOVE!

Here are a few strategies to better pinpoint your strengths and improve your self-awareness:

1. For one to two weeks, draw a line down the middle on a sheet of paper and make a list. On the left side, write down all the things that you enjoyed doing, what you loved, activities that made you the most happy, things you truly excelled at. On the other side, write down another list of things you avoided, procrastinated, and hated doing. This activity should help you narrow your search.

2. Make another list. If money was no object and you were set for life: What would you do with your time? Who would you spend your time with? Who would you serve and help?

3. Ask five people closest to you to tell you the truth about yourself—what do they see as your strengths, what do they think you do well?

4. Check out *StrengthsFinder 2.0* by Tom Rath to help you discover your top five strengths.

5. Still having trouble? Ask yourself this question: "What am I curious about?" This is the advice frequently offered by the author of *Eat Pray Love*, Elizabeth Gilbert. Many people have a tough time identifying what their clear passion is. That is OK, and perfectly normal. Gilbert advises a different strategy. "Instead of being anxious about chasing a passion that you're not even feeling, do something that's a lot simpler, just follow your curiosity." Once you tap into that curiosity: experiment, fail, learn, practice. Over time, that curiosity can lead to something amazing.

Utilize one of, if not all of, these tools to do more of what you love at work, or to start a new path of fulfillment by focusing on your strengths. Whether you complete the tasks listed above or not, I encourage you to answer the four questions below to steer yourself in the right direction to live a life that you love:

What are your strengths (what are you good at)?

What comes naturally to you and gives you energy?

What brings you joy at work or school (how can you do more of this)?

What areas or topics in life are you curious about? (This might help you discover your passion.)

Here's some motivation for you. You have only one life to live! How are you going to spend your one shot: surviving or thriving? It's time to THRIVE. Take the time to answer the questions above and use those answers to spend more time developing, enhancing, and focusing on what you love to do. Start leveraging your strengths today.

PART III: LOVE THE LITTLE THINGS

The human species is one of the only species on the planet that can laugh. Yet, so many people walk around each day like zombies because either they a) are stressed and miserable because they hate what they are doing, or b) ungrateful and have a hard time recognizing how truly blessed they are. The life skill of recognizing all the beauty that is around us is truly a talent that takes practice, but once it is mastered, will create a great deal of momentum that fosters joy and happiness.

So how do we find this joy? What practices can we adopt to achieve inner peace and a sense of fulfillment? Real estate investor, trainer, and New York Times bestselling author Dean Graziosi offers a unique perspective while speaking on Lewis Howes' podcast, *The School of Greatness*. He suggests, "lower your standards" on what fills you with gratitude. When I first heard this I was taken aback. When has lowering my standards ever helped me? Well, like many high achievers, go-getters, and competitive people, we are looking to be the best, so we set the bar high. Many of us, including myself for a very long time, fell into the trap shared by Ricky Bobby, "If you ain't first, you're last." This type of mindset fosters the tendency to lose sight of what really matters: improving ourselves daily, contributing to others, and being thankful in all things.

A great foundational starting point is to look at all situations with a lens of gratitude (see Chapter 9). This mindset will shift your feelings and focus to finding the good in all things. There are moments when things go wrong and we fail. Feeling frustrated and upset is perfectly normal. Instead of feeling like a victim though, look for the learning opportunity and use it to grow. Let that failure fuel you to improve.

INSTEAD OF HAVING THE CONSTANT NEED TO PROVE YOURSELF, TRY TO FOCUS ON IMPROVING YOURSELF.

RIDE ALONG

As part of my role as a sales professional and sales trainer, I have the opportunity to ride with new reps and candidates. As these work trips usually go, the potential employee asks questions about the job as they try to gain more information about the products, get insights on customer concerns, and learn what the day-to-day looks like. Often these individuals are jotting down notes in their journals and formulating a plan to knock out their final interview while putting their best foot forward in hopes that I sing their praises to the hiring manager.

On one particular day, I had an interesting conversation with a candidate. Most of the day went as usual: visiting accounts, answering questions, explaining the industry, and so on. But this time, the candidate—let's call her Stacy—asked me a great question. She asked, "If there is one thing I need to know, one piece of advice you can give me to crush this job, what is it?"

I thought about it for a second, while driving past the old battleships nestled in the waters of Bremerton, Washington. I pondered the question, thinking of the right response that would genuinely help her. The standard answer would be to uncover a customer need, use active listening skills, master your products and disease state, work really hard, bring value, and ask for the business. Deep down I felt that response would be just like those old war vessels...rusty and outdated.

For some reason, that day was different. Those of you who have followed my blog *Project Rise* may have witnessed a dramatic shift in my mindset that I'm trying to share in this book. This process has fostered an intellectual journey that has been one of the most transformational forces in my life. It has taught me a powerful act of vulnerability. The process of sharing my thoughts, research, opinions, and strategies has been truly rewarding. I have learned that I don't have to create but document my journey. As I mentioned in an earlier chapter, I am working on developing an Improve Mindset—focusing on the process, learning, and growing; not simply on outcomes and the black and whiteness of a win or a loss. For most of my life I was living with a Prove Mindset—gaining my self-worth and validation by proving to myself and others that I was good enough.

Trust me, I'm still a work in progress, but this time, when asked for advice on succeeding, I wanted to share something different. I simply told Stacy:

JUST KNOW THAT YOU ARE ALIVE…
YOU ARE ALIVE!

Someone who doesn't know me might think, "Man, this dude is corny. Definitely on the cheesy side." You know what, I really don't care. I wanted her to know then and you to know now that you are ALIVE! Be grateful and take advantage of this precious gift of having the freedom of being present, here, alive today. To think, to act, and to do whatever it is that you want.

Most people wake up each day and take for granted all the possibilities being alive has to offer. Seriously, why do people wait? For some it takes surviving a traumatic event or threat of loss to truly appreciate how insanely lucky we are to experience just a single day and all the possibilities and wonders each moment brings. Don't make a loss make you finally live.

MY LIST

We take for granted the small things, which really are the BIG THINGS. Get ready for my random list of small pleasures:

Hearing a child's laughter, going on a walk and feeling the wind in my face, a grilled cheese sandwich with bacon, going to the movies, reading a good book, smelling a scent that takes me back, experiencing the sunrise on a morning run, waking up on a Saturday morning to ESPN College Gameday, going to the gym, picking raspberries with my kids, physical touch from a loved one…. The list can go on and on.

How would you live your life if you knew you only had three

197

months to live? Would that change how you thought, acted, lived, and loved? What would you appreciate more if you had just be released from prison after being locked up for 20 years?

I had the opportunity to play softball a few years ago with a group of federal inmates. While there, I spoke to one of my former classmates who had 10 more years to serve in prison. Wow, what insight I gained. The freedoms we recognize if we change our lens are so immense and beautiful. Are we living with the perspective of gratitude? Are we maximizing all the wonderful resources we have at our disposal?

Living today, right now, I truly feel blessed...blessed and motivated to do as much as I can while I'm here.

Sometimes I feel like singer John Mayer in his song, "Stop This Train"...so *I play the numbers game, to find a way to say my life has just begun.* If I do the math, I have about two-thirds of my life left, and that's if I live to be 100. This is a long-winded way of reminding the candidate in my car, you, and even myself that if you are reading this: YOU ARE ALIVE, BUT ARE YOU TRULY LIVING?

We get only ONE SHOT at life. This is my plea to you—and still to myself—to do a few things right now:
- Love more, judge less
- Laugh at yourself, not at others
- Cry TOJ—tears of joy
- Think deeply and independently
- See beauty in all things
- Find gratitude even in hardships and setbacks
- Ask yourself this question at the end of each day: "How many people did I help?"
- Know that you are only limited by your thoughts
- Do and be anything you want—it all starts and ends in your mind
- Be generous
- Remember that forgiveness transcends
- Know and use these words often: "please" and "thank you"
- Fight the battles ahead, not the ones behind you

• Plan for the future, but be present today

Lastly, believe in yourself. You are special. You are a miracle. Since you are a miracle, make and recognize mini-miracles daily. And know that God loves you just the way you are, so just be yourself.

Live the life you dream about. Do not wait for an event to force you into action. Make this powerful choice now. Chose to love yourself, do more of what you love to do, and recognize the beauty all around you.

Happiness is not about money, but moments. Fulfillment isn't found in status, but service. Joy is not achieved by acquiring things, but in harnessing the power of thankfulness. This approach is my best practice. This is the advice that I gave Stacy and now you. I hope that you take it, run with it, and never look back.

RISE REVIEW

In Summary:
1. Love yourself.
2. Do more activities that you love to do at work or school—make this strength your career!
3. Be intentional about finding the little things in everyday life that create the feeling of love, gratitude, and joy.

If you can do these three things, there is nothing that can stop you from RISING. This approach will give you more energy and passion to be the best version of you. You owe it to yourself and others to take care of yourself first before you can effectively take care of others.

PROJECT RISE

200

IN CLOSING

Have you seen the award winning documentary film *Gleason*? If not, check it out on Amazon. It's a must-see. It chronicles former NFL special teams standout Steve Gleason's diagnosis and journey living with ALS. It is one of the most raw, vulnerable, courageous, and moving films I have ever seen.

I had the privilege of playing football with Steve for one season at WSU. The hardest hit I ever took wasn't in a game, but during practice. I caught a slant over the middle and Steve blindsided me, knocking me five feet in the air. Luckily, I was able get back up (though my ear was ringing for two hours after that hit).

Steve, his wife Michel, and their son, Rivers, get back up every single day. Their family is a true inspiration to me and to millions of others who know their story.

Steve's outlook and attitude while living with ALS is a reminder to me to live with vision and purpose...and to not waste a single day.

How would you live if you knew you only had six months before your body was going to fail you? What would you say if you knew you wouldn't be able to speak because your vocal cords stopped working? What actions and adventures would you take if you knew you won't be able to walk again?

For me, the eight habits I share in this book are a great place to start:

1. Set goals
2. Document your vision by writing your thoughts, intentions, and feelings down
3. Be grateful

4. Determine a clear objective each day
5. Love yourself through affirmations
6. Learn something new daily
7. Help and serve others
8. Visualize and dream often

The only speech I remember from my freshman season was from Steve. His message to the team was to Dream Big. Without a shadow of doubt, Steve still lives by that creed, and I hope you do too.

THANK YOU

I am so grateful for having the opportunity to share these thoughts and ideas with you. I am also thankful that you have gotten this far. Keep this energy going; create a new process for yourself and make sure to trust that process. The legendary Hall of Fame football coach from Pacific Lutheran University, Frosty Westering, teaches us in his book, *Make the Big Time Where You Are*, it's not the "road to success," it is the "success road." We are never a completed product, but one that continually builds and gets better every day.

I am so excited for you and for what lies ahead. I see a RISE on the horizon that is so amazing and full of abundance that you will be wishing you would have learned these techniques years ago. Well, it's never too late. You are never too young or too old. The time is NOW! Live the life you've always dreamed of. Do the things you've only imagined. Take control of your destiny. It all starts with your mindset.

Commit to yourself, as well as the ones you love, to stick with this daily journaling system for at least seven days. Come up with ways to hold yourself accountable—whether it's rewarding yourself in some way or figuring out a way to reprimand yourself if you don't finish—just figure out a system that works best for you and do it.

Once you have completed the *Rise Journal 7 Day Challenge*, keep the momentum moving by going to www.theCollinHenderson.com and get your *Rise Journal*. This journal will help you revisit your goals and continue to keep your habits of practicing gratitude, identifying your one objective, affirming yourself, learning new things, serving others, and visualizing.

**IT'S TIME TO RISE UP AND BE THE
BEST VERSION OF YOU.**

**GO OUT AND DO IT,
FOR THE BEST IS YET TO COME.**

ACKNOWLEDGMENTS

My first and most important THANK YOU goes to my amazing best friend and wife, Kendra. My journey could not be possible without you. I wake up each day with the biggest grin and feelings of gratitude knowing that I have the privilege of living each day side by side with you. My love for you knows no ends or bounds. You are truly the best version of me.

Also, I have to give a big shout out (and hugs and kisses) to my main source of inspiration—my children—Baylor, Bellamy, Winnie, and Norah. Just know that daddy loves you so much and that I RISE each day to help create a world and a father that you are proud of.

A much deserved thank you goes to my mom, dad, and my big bro—P. Hen! Thank you for all your love and support throughout my entire life. Saying that you have blessed me deeply would be an understatement. I have to also give a huge thank you to my in-laws: Tammy and Ray. Thank you for loving me like a son, teaching me like a mentor, and having fun with me like a best friend. Oh, and I can't forget my sissie's Mera and Chelsey—I love you both!

To all of my coaches, teachers, managers, teammates, family and friends, thank you for shaping me into the person that I am today. I love you all and hope this book will be a catalyst to rekindle these much valued relationships. A huge shout out goes to my favorite coach I've ever had—Coach Price. Thank you so much for your love, leadership, and for writing an amazing forward to this book. Thanks to Mike Mersinger and Tom Couture for hiring me. My life truly changed on that fateful day.

A big thank you goes to my editors: Susan Henderson, Rachel Johnson, Kristin Sierra, and Kate Bethell. Thanks for making me look better than I am. Thanks G. Biz for the book publishing guidance. Much love to Destiny Ostrander and Natalie Narayan for your much valued additions and contributions throughout my writing process. Props to the book cover art designer and format-ter: my amazing bride, Kendra. The time, energy, and love you all put into the words that are on these pages is deeply appreciated and this book would not be possible without your contribution.

I love you all,
Collin

SUGGESTED READING
IN ORDER OF REFERENCE
IN THIS BOOK

There is one thing I know to be true—my life did not transform until I went ALL IN on my personal development. As I mentioned earlier in the book, my mentor Frankie Pretzel gave me a list of books to read one day, and that list changed my life. I wanted what he had. Thus, I took that list, and made time to digest and absorb knowledge and best practices of the world's brightest minds. This one step of committing to my learning is why I am writing this book.

You owe it to yourself to invest in your development, knowledge, and skill. Make learning, reading, and listening to successful people a daily habit. Download audiobooks or podcasts to listen to while you drive or workout. Carve out time in either the morning or evening to read 15-30 minutes a day. You will not get big-time results unless you fill your brain with the nutrients and wisdom needed to progress and grow. Successful people do what others are not willing to do.

On the next few pages I share a list of the books that I referenced in *Project Rise*. My challenge to you is to pick three from this list and read or listen to them. These books changed my life, and I hope they'll do the same for you. This is just the tip of the iceberg though. Make lifelong learning the ace up your sleeve. Take charge of your life by taking control of your development. If you commit to checking these books off your list of reads, I GUARANTEE your life will change forever.

Mindset: The New Psychology of Success by Carol Dweck (Random House Publishing Group, 2006)

Confidence: How to Overcome Your Limiting Beliefs and Achieve Your Goals by Martin Meadows (Meadows Publishing, 2015)

Positive Intelligence: Why Only 20% of Teams and Individuals Achieve Their True Potential AND HOW YOU CAN ACHIEVE YOURS by Shirzad Chamine (Greenleaf Book Group, LLC, 2012)

The End of Stress: Four Steps to Rewire Your Brain by Don Joseph Goewey (Atria Books/Beyond Words, 2014)

No Excuses!: The Power of Self-Discipline for Success in Your Life by Brian Tracy (Da Capo Books, 2011)

Think and Grow Rich by Napoleon Hill (International Alliance Pro-Publishing, LLC, 2010)

The 10X Rule: The Only Difference Between Success and Failure by Grant Cardone (John Wiley & Sons, Inc., 2011)

The School of Greatness: A Real-World Guide to Living Bigger, Loving Deeper, and Leaving a Legacy by Lewis Howes (Rodale Press, Inc., 2015)

9 Things Successful People Do Differently by Heidi Grant Halvorson (Harvard Business Review Press, 2012)

Grit: The Power of Passion and Persistence by Angela Duckworth (Scribner, 2016)

Start with Why by Simon Sinek (Penguin Publishing Group, 2009)

18 Minutes: Find Your Focus, Master Distraction, and Get the Right Things Done by Peter Bregman (Grand Central Publishing, 2011)

The Power of Habit: Why We Do What We Do in Life and Business by Charles Duhigg (Random House Publishing Group, 2012)

The Happiness Advantage: The Seven Principles of Positive Psychology That Fuel Success and Performance at Work by Shawn Achor (The Crown Publishing Group, 2010)

The ONE Thing: The Surprisingly Simple Truth Behind Extraordinary Results by Gary Keller and Jay Papasan (Bard Press TX, 2013)

The Energy Bus: 10 Rules to Fuel Your Life, Work, and Team with Positive Energy by Jon Gordon (John Wiley & Sons Inc 2007)

The Obstacle is the Way: The Timeless Art of Turning Trials into Triumph by Ryan Holiday (Penguin Publishing Group, 2014)

Successful Advertising. 1885 by Thomas Smith

The Secret by Rhonda Byrne (Gardners Books 2006)

Lead Like Jesus: Lessons from the Greatest Leadership Role Model of All Time by Ken Blanchard and Phil Hodges (Nelson, Thomas, Inc., 2006)

The Hidden Gifts of Helping: How the Power of Giving, Compassion, and Hope Can Get Us Through Hard Times by Stephen G. Post (John Wiley & Sons, Inc., 2011)

Ego Is the Enemy by Ryan Holiday (Penguin Publishing Group, 2016)

Tools For Titans: The Tactics, Routines, and Habits of Billionaires, Icons, and World-Class Performers by Tim Ferriss (Houghton Mifflin Harcourt, 2016)

The Alchemist: A Fable About Following Your Dream by Paulo Coelho (HarperCollins Publishers, 1993)

Captivate: The Science of Succeeding with People by Vanessa Van Edwards (Penguin Publishing Group, 2017)

StrengthsFinder 2.0 by Tom Rath (Gallup Press, 2007)

Make the Big Time Where You Are by Frosty Westering (Big Five Productions, 2001)

RISE JOURNAL
SEVEN DAY CHALLENGE

All athletes warm up their bodies before competition. Singers warm up their voice before they perform. Race car drivers warm up their engines before each race. You can't bake a pie or a pizza without preheating the oven. In order to get the change and focus you are looking for, you too need to warm up and PRIME your mindset before you begin each day. This system only takes five to ten minutes a day...seriously, that's it!

You can work on your *Rise Journal* before you go to sleep at night, before you get up in the morning, or a combination of both (half in the morning and half before you go to bed)...it really doesn't matter. See an example on the next page.

Now it's your turn to make journaling a keystone habit that creates the clarity needed to perform at your best. Writing your thoughts, intentions, and feelings down have been scientifically proven to reduce stress, improve happiness, and increase the likelihood of achieving your goals. Good luck...I know you can do it!

Once you complete the *Rise Journal Seven Day Challenge*, visit my website to purchase a *Rise Journal* and continue this winning habit.

WWW.THECOLLINHENDERSON.COM

G.O.A.L.S. V. Sept 15, 2017
RISE JOURNAL EXAMPLE

G   I am so grateful that I get to take Baylor to preschool today and pick him up. I love seeing that smile on his face.

O   Finish my expense report and turn it in my 5pm.

A   I have everything I need to finish the year #1. I've put in the work and I'm off to a great start. I'm deserving of being a champion!

L   I can't wait to listen to more of the Little Red Book of Selling today in my car. I learned a key tactic yesterday on the power of using visuals to enhance the buying experience.

S   I'm going to bring home flowers today for Kendra. I know this will make her day!

V   I am a New York Times Bestselling author and by 2020 I have impacted twenty million lives somehow in a positive way.

G.O.A.L.S. V.

GRATITUDE. OBJECTIVE. AFFIRMATION. LEARN. SERVE. VISUALIZE.

G _____

_____

O _____

_____

A _____

_____

L _____

_____

S _____

_____

V _____

_____

G.O.A.L.S. V.

GRATITUDE. OBJECTIVE. AFFIRMATION. LEARN. SERVE. VISUALIZE.

G _____

_____

O _____

_____

A _____

_____

L _____

_____

S _____

_____

V _____

_____

G.O.A.L.S. V.

GRATITUDE. OBJECTIVE. AFFIRMATION. LEARN. SERVE. VISUALIZE.

G _____

_____

O _____

_____

A _____

_____

L _____

_____

S _____

_____

V _____

_____

G.O.A.L.S. V.

GRATITUDE. OBJECTIVE. AFFIRMATION. LEARN. SERVE. VISUALIZE.

G _____

_____

O _____

_____

A _____

_____

L _____

_____

S _____

_____

V _____

_____

G.O.A.L.S. V.

GRATITUDE. OBJECTIVE. AFFIRMATION. LEARN. SERVE. VISUALIZE.

G _____

_____

O _____

_____

A _____

_____

L _____

_____

S _____

_____

V _____

_____

G.O.A.L.S. V.

GRATITUDE. OBJECTIVE. AFFIRMATION. LEARN. SERVE. VISUALIZE.

G _____

_____

O _____

_____

A _____

_____

L _____

_____

S _____

_____

V _____

_____

G.O.A.L.S. V.

GRATITUDE. OBJECTIVE. AFFIRMATION. LEARN. SERVE. VISUALIZE.

G _____

_____

O _____

_____

A _____

_____

L _____

_____

S _____

_____

V _____

_____

ABOUT THE AUTHOR
COLLIN HENDERSON

Collin and his wife Kendra Henderson live near Seattle, Washington, with their four children: Baylor, Bellamy, Winnie, and Norah. Collin was a dual sport student-athlete and Academic All-American at Washington State University, playing both football and baseball. He received his undergraduate degree and master's in Education at WSU (Go Cougs!). Collin has been an award-winning sales professional for over 10 years in the medical sales industry for two Fortune 500 companies as a representative and sales trainer.

In February of 2016, Collin launched his blog *Project Rise* and enjoys researching, writing, and speaking to organizations, schools, teams, and individuals about mastering your mindset and performing at your best.

TO BOOK COLLIN TO SPEAK TO YOUR GROUP OR AT YOUR EVENT, PLEASE VISIT:

WWW.THECOLLINHENDERSON.COM

Made in the USA
San Bernardino, CA
21 June 2018